For
Business
Students

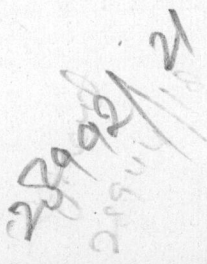

HBR's 10 Must Reads series is the definitive collection of ideas and best practices for aspiring and experienced leaders alike. These books offer essential reading selected from the pages of *Harvard Business Review* on topics critical to the success of every manager.

Titles include:

For Business Students

HARVARD BUSINESS REVIEW PRESS

Boston, Massachusetts

Printed in India by Replika Press Pvt. Ltd.
10 9 8 7 6 5 4 3

The web addresses referenced in this book were live and correct at the time of the book's publication but may be subject to change.

Cataloging-in-Publication data is forthcoming.

ISBN: 978-1-64782-587-4
eISBN: 978-1-64782-588-1

MIX
Paper | Supporting
responsible forestry
FSC
www.fsc.org   FSC™ C016779

Contents

For
Business
Students

Manage Your Work, Manage Your Life

Zero in on what really matters.

by Boris Groysberg and Robin Abrahams

WORK/LIFE BALANCE IS at best an elusive ideal and at worst a complete myth, today's senior executives will tell you. But by making deliberate choices about which opportunities they'll pursue and which they'll decline, rather than simply reacting to emergencies, leaders can and do engage meaningfully with work, family, and community. They've discovered through hard experience that prospering in the senior ranks is a matter of carefully combining work and home so as not to lose themselves, their loved ones, or their foothold on success. Those who do this most effectively involve their families in work decisions and activities. They also vigilantly manage their own human capital, endeavoring to give both work and home their due—over a period of years, not weeks or days.

That's how the 21st-century business leaders in our research said they reconcile their professional and personal lives. In this article we draw on five years' worth of interviews with almost 4,000 executives worldwide, conducted by students at Harvard Business School, and a survey of 82 executives in an HBS leadership course.

Deliberate choices don't guarantee complete control. Life sometimes takes over, whether it's a parent's dementia or a teenager's car accident. But many of the executives we've studied—men and women alike—have sustained their momentum during such challenges while staying connected to their families. Their stories and advice reflect five main themes: defining success for yourself, managing technology, building support networks at work and at home, traveling or relocating selectively, and collaborating with your partner.

Defining Success for Yourself

When you are leading a major project, you determine early on what a win should look like. The same principle applies to leading a deliberate life: You have to define what success means to you—understanding, of course, that your definition will evolve over time.

Executives' definitions of professional and personal success run a gamut from the tactical to the conceptual (see the exhibit "How Leaders Define Work/Life 'Wins'"). For one leader, it means being home at least four nights a week. For another, it means understanding what's going on in the lives of family members. For a third, it's about having emotional energy at both work and home.

Some intriguing gender differences emerged in our survey data: In defining professional success, women place more value than men do on individual achievement, having passion for their work, receiving respect, and making a difference, but less value on organizational achievement and ongoing learning and development. A lower percentage of women than of men list financial achievement as an aspect of personal or professional success. Rewarding relationships are by far the most common element of personal success for both sexes, but men list merely having a family as an indicator of success, whereas women describe what a good family life looks like to them. Women are also more likely to mention the importance of friends and community as well as family.

The survey responses consisted of short phrases and lists, but in the interviews executives often defined personal success by telling a story or describing an ideal self or moment in time. Such narratives and self-concepts serve as motivational goalposts, helping people prioritize activities and make sense of conflicts and inconsistencies.

When work and family responsibilities collide, for example, men may lay claim to the cultural narrative of the good provider.

Idea in Brief

The Problem

Senior executives in this generation feel they can't achieve "balance" through constant juggling, which prevents them from engaging meaningfully either at work or at home.

The Solution

They find that they're more focused—and effective—when they make deliberate choices about which opportunities to pursue in both realms.

The Outcome

Leaders who carefully manage their own human capital in this way maintain a higher degree of satisfaction professionally and personally.

Several male executives who admitted to spending inadequate time with their families consider absence an acceptable price for providing their children with opportunities they themselves never had. One of these men, poor during his childhood, said that his financial success both protects his children and validates his parents' struggles. Another even put a positive spin on the breakup of his family: "Looking back, I would have still made a similar decision to focus on work, as I was able to provide for my family and become a leader in my area, and these things were important to me. Now I focus on my kids' education . . . and spend a lot more time with them over weekends."

Even the men who pride themselves on having achieved some degree of balance between work and other realms of their lives measure themselves against a traditional male ideal. "The 10 minutes I give my kids at night is one million times greater than spending that 10 minutes at work," one interviewee said. It's difficult to imagine a woman congratulating herself for spending 10 minutes a day with her children, but a man may consider the same behavior exemplary.

Indeed, women rarely view themselves as working *for* their families the way men do. Men still think of their family responsibilities in terms of breadwinning, whereas women often see theirs as role modeling for their children. Women emphasize (far more than men do) how important it is for their kids—particularly their daughters—to

How leaders define work/life "wins"

In their definitions of professional and personal success, executives highlight these elements:

Professional success means…

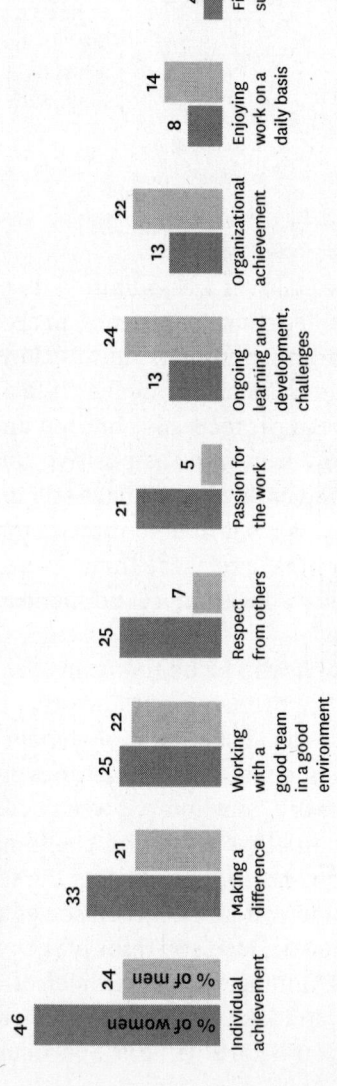

	% of women	% of men
Individual achievement	46	24
Making a difference	33	21
Working with a good team in a good environment	25	22
Respect from others	25	7
Passion for the work	21	5
Ongoing learning and development, challenges	13	24
Organizational achievement	13	22
Enjoying work on a daily basis	8	14
Financial success	4	16

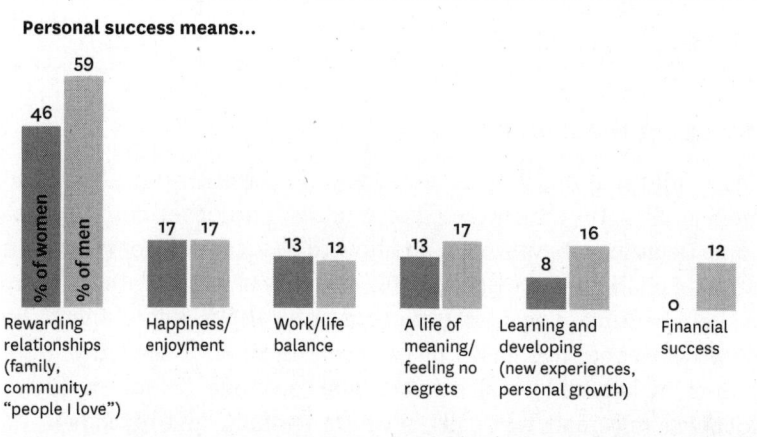

Personal success means...

% of women
% of men

46 / 59	17 / 17	13 / 12	13 / 17	8 / 16	0 / 12
Rewarding relationships (family, community, "people I love")	Happiness/ enjoyment	Work/life balance	A life of meaning/ feeling no regrets	Learning and developing (new experiences, personal growth)	Financial success

see them as competent professionals. One said, "I think that work is such a big part of who I am. I want my kids to understand what I do. I am a whole being."

Many women said that the most difficult aspect of managing work and family is contending with cultural expectations about mothering. One admitted that she stopped working at home after her daughter referred to the Bloomberg network as "Mommy's channel." Another commented, "When you are paid well, you can get all the [practical] help you need. What is the most difficult thing, though—what I see my women friends leave their careers for—is the real emotional guilt of not spending enough time with their children. The guilt of *missing out.*"

Both men and women expressed versions of this guilt and associated personal success with not having regrets. They often cope by assigning special significance to a particular metric, such as never missing a Little League game or checking in once a day no matter what. "I just prioritize dinner with my family as if it was a 6 PM meeting with my most important client," said one interviewee. Another offered this suggestion: "Design your house right—have a table in the kitchen where your kids can do homework while your husband cooks and you drink a glass of red wine." Though expressed as advice, this is clearly her very personal, concrete image of what success at home looks like.

Managing Technology

Nearly all the interviewees talked about how critical it is to corral their emails, text messages, voice mails, and other communications. Deciding when, where, and how to be accessible for work is an ongoing challenge, particularly for executives with families. Many of them cautioned against using communications technology to be in two places at once, insisting on the value of undivided attention. "When I'm at home, I really am at home," said one. "I force myself to not check my email, take calls, et cetera. I want to give my kids 100% of my attention. But this also works the other way around, because when I'm at work I really want to focus on work. I believe that mixing these spheres too much leads to confusion and mistakes."

That last point is a common concern: Always being plugged in can erode performance. One leader observed that "certain cognitive processes happen when you step away from the frenetic responding to emails." (The history of science, after all, is marked by insights that occurred not in the laboratory but while the scientist was engaged in a mundane task—or even asleep.) Another executive pointed out that 24-hour availability can actually hamper initiative in an organization: "If you have weak people who must ask your advice all the time, you feel important. But there is a difference between being truly important and just not letting anyone around you do anything without you."

Strikingly, some people at the top are starting to use communications technology less often while they're working. Several invoked the saying "You can't raise a kid by phone"—and pointed out that it's not the best way to manage a team, either. Often, if it's logistically possible, you're better off communicating in person. How do you know when that's the case? One interviewee made an important distinction between broadcasting information and exchanging and analyzing ideas: "Speaking [on the phone] is easy, but careful,

What partners contribute

Executives say that their partners and spouses share their vision of success, bring complementary skills, and provide the following types of support:

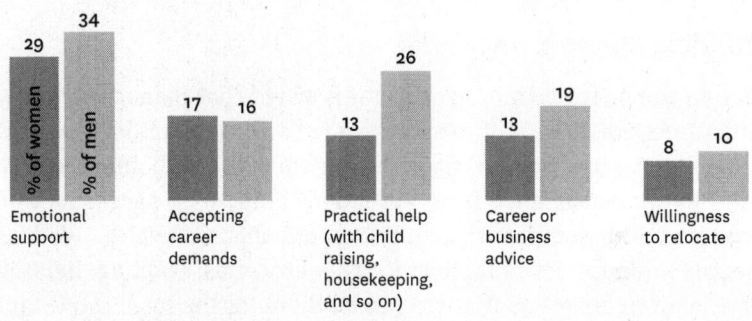

Both camps—those who hate being plugged in and those who love it—acknowledged that executives must learn to manage communications technology wisely. Overall, they view it as a good servant

thoughtful listening becomes very challenging. For the most important conversations, I see a real trend moving back to face-to-face. When you're evaluating multibillion-dollar deals . . . you have to build a bridge to the people."

When it comes to technology in the home, more than a third of the surveyed executives view it as an invader, and about a quarter see it as a liberator. (The rest are neutral or have mixed feelings.) Some of them resent the smartphone's infringement on family time: "When your phone buzzes," one ruefully noted, it's difficult to "keep your eyes on that soccer field." Others appreciate the flexibility that technology affords them: "I will probably leave here around 4 PM to wrangle my kids," said one participant, "but I will be back and locked into my network and emails by 8 PM." Another participant reported, "Sometimes my kids give me a hard time about being on my BlackBerry at the dinner table, but I tell them that my BlackBerry is what enables me to be home with them."

Both camps—those who hate being plugged in and those who love it—acknowledged that executives must learn to manage communications technology wisely. Overall, they view it as a good servant but a bad master. Their advice in this area is quite consistent: Make yourself available but not *too* available to your team; be honest with yourself about how much you can multitask; build relationships and trust through face time; and keep your in-box under control.

Building Support Networks

Across the board, senior executives insisted that managing family and professional life requires a strong network of behind-the-scenes supporters. Absent a primary caregiver who stays at home, they see paid help or assistance from extended family as a necessity. The women in our sample are adamant about this. One said, "We hire people to do the more tactical things—groceries, cooking, helping the children dress—so that we can be there for the most important things." Even interviewees without children said they needed support at home when they became responsible for aging parents or suffered their own health problems.

Emotional support is equally essential. Like anyone else, executives occasionally need to vent when they're dealing with something crazy or irritating at work, and friends and family are a safer audience than colleagues. Sometimes leaders also turn to their personal networks for a fresh perspective on a problem or a decision, because members of their teams don't always have the distance to be objective.

Support at work matters too. Trusted colleagues serve as valuable sounding boards. And many leaders reported that health crises—their own or family members'—might have derailed their careers if not for compassionate bosses and coworkers. The unexpected can waylay even the most carefully planned career.

"When you're young, you think you can control everything," one interviewee said, "but you can't." Executives told stories about heart attacks, cancer, and parents in need of care. One talked about a psychotic reaction to medication. In those situations, mentors and team members helped leaders weather difficult times and eventually return to business as usual.

What about mixing personal and professional networks, since executives must draw on both anyway? That's up for discussion.

The men we surveyed tend to prefer separate networks, and the women are pretty evenly split. Interviewees who favor integration said it's a relief to be "the same person" in all contexts and natural to form friendships at work, where they spend most of their time. Those who separate their work lives from their private lives have many reasons for doing so. Some seek novelty and a counterbalance to work. "If all of your socializing centers around your work life, you tend to experience an ever-decreasing circle of influence and ideas," one pointed out. Others want to protect their personal relationships from the churn of the workplace.

Many women keep their networks separate for fear of harming their image. Some never mention their families at work because they don't want to appear unprofessional. A few female executives won't discuss their careers—or even mention that they have jobs—in conversations outside work. But again, not all women reported such conflict between their professional and personal "selves," and several suggested that the tide is turning. One pointed out, "The more women have come into the workplace, the more I talk about my children."

Traveling or Relocating Selectively

Discussions about work/life balance usually focus on managing time. But it's also critical to manage your location—and, more broadly, your role in the global economy. When leaders decide whether to travel or relocate (internationally or domestically), their home lives play a huge part. That's why many of them believe in acquiring global experience and racking up travel miles while they're young and unencumbered. Of those surveyed, 32% said they had turned down an international assignment because they did not want to relocate their families, and 28% said they had done so to protect their marriages.

Several executives told stories about getting sidetracked or derailed in their careers because a partner or spouse needed to relocate. Of course, travel becomes even trickier with children. Many women reported cutting back on business trips after having children, and several executives of both sexes said they had refused to relocate when their children were adolescents. "When children are very young, they are more mobile," one explained. "But once they are 12 or 13, they want to be in one place."

Female executives are less likely than men to be offered or accept international assignments, in part because of family responsibilities but also because of the restrictive gender roles in certain cultures or perceptions that they are unwilling to relocate. Our survey results—from a well-traveled sample—jibe with student interviewers' qualitative findings. Almost none of the men surveyed (less than 1%, compared with 13% of the women) had turned down an international assignment because of cultural concerns. But for female executives, not all travel is created equal: Gender norms, employment laws, health-care access, and views on work/life balance vary from country to country. One American woman said it requires extra effort in Europe to make sure she doesn't "come off as being intimidating," a concern she attributes in part to being tall. Another woman said that in the Middle East she has had to bring male colleagues to meetings to prove her credibility.

Though women in particular have such difficulties, international assignments are not easy for anyone, and they may simply not be worth it for many executives. Members of both sexes have built gratifying careers while grounding themselves in a particular country or even city. However, if travel is undesirable, ambitious young executives should decide so early on. That way they can avoid getting trapped in an industry that doesn't mesh with their geographic preferences and give themselves time to find ways other than travel to signal open-mindedness, sophistication, skill diversity, and willingness to go above and beyond. (Several executives noted that international experience is often viewed as a sign of those personal attributes.) "International experience can be helpful," one executive observed, "but it's just as important to have had exposure across the business lines. Both allow you to understand that not everybody thinks as you do." Some executives even question the future of globe-hopping, noting that carbon costs, fuel costs, and security concerns may tighten future travel budgets.

Collaborating with Your Partner

Managing yourself, technology, networks, travel—it's a tall order. Leaders with strong family lives spoke again and again of needing a shared vision of success for everyone at home—not just for themselves. Most of the executives in our sample have partners or spouses, and common goals hold those couples together. Their relationships offer both partners opportunities—for uninterrupted (or less interrupted) work, for adventurous travel, for intensive parenting, for political or community impact—that they might not otherwise have had.

Leaders also emphasized the importance of complementary relationships. Many said how much they value their partners' emotional intelligence, task focus, big-picture thinking, detail orientation—in short, whatever cognitive or behavioral skills balance out their own tendencies. And many of those we surveyed consider emotional support the biggest contribution their partners have made to their careers. Both men and women often mentioned that their partners believe in them or have urged them to take business risks or pursue job opportunities that were not immediately rewarding but led to longer-term satisfaction. They also look to their partners to be sounding boards and honest critics. One executive said that her partner asks "probing questions to challenge my thinking so I can be better prepared for an opposing viewpoint."

A partner's support may come in many forms, but what it almost always boils down to is making sure the executive manages his or her own human capital effectively. The pressures and demands on executives are intense, multidirectional, and unceasing. Partners can help them keep their eyes on what matters, budget their time and energy, live healthfully, and make deliberate choices—sometimes tough ones—about work, travel, household management, and community involvement.

Men, however, appear to be getting more spousal support overall. Male interviewees—many of whom have stay-at-home wives—often spoke of their spouses' willingness to take care of children, tolerate long work hours, and even relocate, sometimes as a way of life.

About the Research

SINCE 2008 MORE THAN 600 students in Harvard Business School's second-year Managing Human Capital course have interviewed 3,850 C-suite executives and leaders (of whom 655 were CEOs, presidents, or board members) at companies and nonprofits around the world.

The goal? To gain greater insight into how today's top leaders make choices in their professional and personal lives. This project has been a true partnership between the students and the executives. Everyone involved wanted to deeply explore what it means for leaders to manage their human capital in the 21st century—and more specifically, in the wake of the recent global recession.

The executives were a diverse group (44% female, 56% male) and represented a wide range of industries, including finance, retail, energy, health care, and technology. They came from 51 countries, and 45% of them had worked in countries other than the United States.

The interviews were semistructured: As long as students related their questions to topics covered in Managing Human Capital, they were allowed considerable leeway in what to ask and how far to go in following up on responses. That way they could dig into the issues they found most compelling.

To supplement the interviews, we surveyed 82 senior executives who were attending a 2012 leadership course at HBS. We asked them about their experiences managing their careers and families. The sample consisted of 58 men and 24 women from 33 countries in Africa, Europe, Asia, the Middle East, and North and South America. Statistics in the article come from the survey data, and quotations come from the field data.

But by and large, they no longer seem to expect the classic 1950s "corporate wife," who hosted dinners for the boss and cocktail parties for clients. (Exceptions exist in some countries and industries. One male executive who works in oil fields said, "When you are living and working in those camp environments, it is indispensable to have your wife talk with other spouses.") Men frequently noted that their partners won't allow them to neglect their families, health, or social lives. For example: "My wife is militant about family dinner, and I am home every night for dinner even if I have to work afterward."

Women, by contrast, slightly more often mentioned their partners' willingness to free them from traditional roles at home. One explained, in a typical comment, "He understands the demands of my role and does not put pressure on me when work takes more time than I would like." In other words, male executives tend to praise their partners for making positive contributions to their careers, whereas women praise theirs for not interfering.

When we look at the survey data, we see other striking differences between the sexes. Fully 88% of the men are married, compared with 70% of the women. And 60% of the men have spouses who don't work full-time outside the home, compared with only 10% of the women. The men have an average of 2.22 children; the women, 1.67.

What Tomorrow's Leaders Think

The fact that the interviewees all agreed to take time from their hectic schedules to share their insights with students might introduce a selection effect. Busy leaders who choose to help students presumably value interpersonal relationships. Because they're inclined to reflect on work and life, they're probably also making deliberate choices in both realms—and they certainly have enough money to pay for support at home. All that may explain why many interviewees reported being basically happy despite their struggles and why few mentioned serious damage to their marriages or families due to career pressures. This sample is an elite group of people better positioned than most to achieve work/life balance. That they nevertheless consider it an impossible task suggests a sobering reality for the rest of us.

Our student interviewers say, almost universally, that the leaders they spoke with dispensed valuable advice about how to maintain both a career and a family. One interviewer reported, "All acknowledged making sacrifices and concessions at times but emphasized the important role that supportive spouses and families played." Still, many students are alarmed at how much leaders sacrifice at home and how little headway the business world has made in adapting to families' needs.

Male executives admitted that they don't prioritize their families enough. And women are more likely than men to have forgone kids or marriage to avoid the pressures of combining work and family. One said, "Because I'm not a mother, I haven't experienced the major driver of inequality: having children." She added, "People assume that if you don't have kids, then you either can't have kids or else you're a hard-driving bitch. So I haven't had any negative career repercussions, but I've probably been judged personally."

Executives of both sexes consider the tension between work and family to be primarily a women's problem, and the students find that discouraging. "Given that leadership positions in corporations around the world are still dominated by men," one explained, "I fear that it will take many organizations much longer than it should to make accommodations for women to . . . effectively manage their careers and personal lives."

Students also resist leaders' commonly held belief that you can't compete in the global marketplace while leading a "balanced" life. When one executive argued that it's impossible to have "a great family life, hobbies, and an amazing career" all at the same time, the student interviewing him initially thought, "That's his perspective." But after more conversations with leaders? "Every single executive confirmed this view in one way or another, and I came to believe that it is the reality of today's business world." It remains to be seen whether, and how, that reality can be changed for tomorrow.

We can't predict what the workplace or the family will look like later in this century, or how the two institutions will coexist. But we can assert three simple truths:

Life happens.

Even the most dedicated executive may suddenly have his or her priorities upended by a personal crisis—a heart attack, for instance, or a death in the family. As one pointed out, people tend to ignore work/life balance until "something is wrong." But that kind of disregard is a choice, and not a wise one. Since when do smart executives assume that everything will work out just fine? If that approach makes no sense in the boardroom or on the factory floor, it makes no sense in one's personal life.

There are multiple routes to success.
Some people plan their careers in detail; others grab whatever opportunity presents itself. Some stick with one company, building political capital and a deep knowledge of the organization's culture and resources; others change employers frequently, relying on external contacts and a fresh perspective to achieve success. Similarly, at home different solutions work for different individuals and families. Some executives have a stay-at-home partner; others make trade-offs to enable both partners to work. The questions of child care, international postings, and smartphones at the dinner table don't have "right" answers. But the questions need to be asked.

No one can do it alone.
Of the many paths to success, none can be walked alone. A support network is crucial both at and outside work—and members of that network must get their needs met too. In pursuit of rich professional and personal lives, men and women will surely continue to face tough decisions about where to concentrate their efforts. Our research suggests that earnestly trying to focus is what will see them through.

Originally published in March 2014. Reprint R1403C

Harnessing the Science of Persuasion

by Robert B. Cialdini

A LUCKY FEW HAVE IT; MOST of us do not. A handful of gifted "naturals" simply know how to capture an audience, sway the undecided, and convert the opposition. Watching these masters of persuasion work their magic is at once impressive and frustrating. What's impressive is not just the easy way they use charisma and eloquence to convince others to do as they ask. It's also how eager those others are to do what's requested of them, as if the persuasion itself were a favor they couldn't wait to repay.

The frustrating part of the experience is that these born persuaders are often unable to account for their remarkable skill or pass it on to others. Their way with people is an art, and artists as a rule are far better at doing than at explaining. Most of them can't offer much help to those of us who possess no more than the ordinary quotient of charisma and eloquence but who still have to wrestle with leadership's fundamental challenge: getting things done through others. That challenge is painfully familiar to corporate executives, who every day have to figure out how to motivate and direct a highly individualistic workforce. Playing the "Because I'm the boss" card is out. Even if it weren't demeaning and demoralizing for all concerned, it would be out of place in a world where cross-functional teams, joint ventures, and intercompany partnerships have blurred the lines of authority. In such an environment, persuasion skills exert far greater influence over others' behavior than formal power structures do.

Which brings us back to where we started. Persuasion skills may be more necessary than ever, but how can executives acquire them if the most talented practitioners can't pass them along? By looking to science. For the past five decades, behavioral scientists have conducted experiments that shed considerable light on the way certain interactions lead people to concede, comply, or change. This research shows that persuasion works by appealing to a limited set of deeply rooted human drives and needs, and it does so in predictable ways. Persuasion, in other words, is governed by basic principles that can be taught, learned, and applied. By mastering these principles, executives can bring scientific rigor to the business of securing consensus, cutting deals, and winning concessions. In the pages that follow, I describe six fundamental principles of persuasion and suggest a few ways that executives can apply them in their own organizations.

The Principle of Liking

People like those who like them.

The application
Uncover real similarities and offer genuine praise.

The retailing phenomenon known as the Tupperware party is a vivid illustration of this principle in action. The demonstration party for Tupperware products is hosted by an individual, almost always a woman, who invites to her home an array of friends, neighbors, and relatives. The guests' affection for their hostess predisposes them to buy from her, a dynamic that was confirmed by a 1990 study of purchase decisions made at demonstration parties. The researchers, Jonathan Frenzen and Harry Davis, writing in the *Journal of Consumer Research*, found that the guests' fondness for their hostess weighed twice as heavily in their purchase decisions as their regard for the products they bought. So when guests at a Tupperware party

Idea in Brief

If leadership, at its most basic, consists of getting things done through others, then persuasion is one of the leader's essential tools. Many executives have assumed that this tool is beyond their grasp, available only to the charismatic and the eloquent. Over the past several decades, though, experimental psychologists have learned which methods reliably lead people to concede, comply, or change. Their research shows that persuasion is governed by several principles that can be taught and applied. The first principle is that people are more likely to follow someone who is similar to them than someone who is not. Wise managers, then, enlist peers to help make their cases. Second, people are more willing to cooperate with those who are not only like them but who like them, as well. So it's worth the time to uncover real similarities and offer genuine praise. Third, experiments confirm the intuitive truth that people tend to treat you the way you treat them. It's sound policy to do a favor before seeking one. Fourth, individuals are more likely to keep promises they make voluntarily and explicitly. The message for managers here is to get commitments in writing. Fifth, studies show that people really do defer to experts. So before they attempt to exert influence, executives should take pains to establish their own expertise and not assume that it's self-evident. Finally, people want more of a commodity when it's scarce; it follows, then, that exclusive information is more persuasive than widely available data. By mastering these principles—and, the author stresses, using them judiciously and ethically—executives can learn the elusive art of capturing an audience, swaying the undecided, and converting the opposition.

buy something, they aren't just buying to please themselves. They're buying to please their hostess as well.

What's true at Tupperware parties is true for business in general: If you want to influence people, win friends. How? Controlled research has identified several factors that reliably increase liking, but two stand out as especially compelling—similarity and praise. Similarity literally draws people together. In one experiment, reported in a 1968 article in the *Journal of Personality*, participants stood physically closer to one another after learning that they shared political beliefs and social values. And in a 1963 article in *American Behavioral Scientists*, researcher F. B. Evans used demographic data

Idea in Practice

Persuasion Principles

Principle	Example	Business application
LIKING: People like those like them, who like them.	At Tupperware parties, guests' fondness for their host influences purchase decisions twice as much as regard for the products.	**To influence people, win friends,** through: *Similarity*: Create *early* bonds with new peers, bosses, and direct reports by informally discovering common interests—you'll establish goodwill and trustworthiness. *Praise*: Charm *and* disarm. Make positive remarks about others—you'll generate more willing compliance.
RECIPROCITY: People repay in kind.	When the Disabled American Veterans enclosed free personalized address labels in donation-request envelops, response rate doubled.	**Give what you want to receive.** Lend a staff member to a colleague who needs help; you'll get *his* help later.
SOCIAL PROOF: People follow the lead of similar others.	More New York City residents tried returning a lost wallet after learning that other New Yorkers had tried.	**Use peer power** to influence horizontally, not vertically; e.g., ask an esteemed "old timer" to support your new initiative if other veterans resist.

from insurance company records to demonstrate that prospects were more willing to purchase a policy from a salesperson who was akin to them in age, religion, politics, or even cigarette-smoking habits.

Managers can use similarities to create bonds with a recent hire, the head of another department, or even a new boss. Informal conversations during the workday create an ideal opportunity to discover at least one common area of enjoyment, be it a hobby, a college basketball team, or reruns of *Seinfeld*. The important thing is to establish the bond early because it creates a presumption of goodwill and trustworthiness in every subsequent encounter. It's much easier to build support for a new project when the people you're trying to persuade are already inclined in your favor.

Principle	Example	Business application
CONSISTENCY: People fulfill written, public, and voluntary commitments.	92% of residents of an apartment complex who signed a petition supporting a new recreation center later donated money to the cause.	**Make others' commitments active, public, and voluntary.** If you supervise an employee who should submit reports on time, get that understanding in writing (a memo); make the commitment public (note colleagues' agreement with the memo); and link the commitment to the employee's values (the impact of timely reports on team spirit).
AUTHORITY: People defer to experts who provide short-cuts to decisions requiring specialized information.	A single *New York Times* expert opinion news story aired on TV generates a 4% shift in U.S. public opinion.	**Don't assume your expertise is self-evident.** Instead, establish your expertise *before* doing business with new colleagues or partners; e.g., in conversations before an important meeting, describe how you solved a problem similar to the one on the agenda.
SCARCITY: People value what's scarce.	Wholesale beef buyers' orders jumped 600% when they alone received information on a possible beef shortage.	**Use exclusive information to persuade.** Influence and rivet key players' attention by saying, for example: ". . . Just got this information today. It won't be distributed until next week."

Praise, the other reliable generator of affection, both charms and disarms. Sometimes the praise doesn't even have to be merited. Researchers at the University of North Carolina writing in the *Journal of Experimental Social Psychology* found that men felt the greatest regard for an individual who flattered them unstintingly even if the comments were untrue. And in their book *Interpersonal Attraction* (Addison-Wesley, 1978), Ellen Berscheid and Elaine Hatfield Walster presented experimental data showing that positive remarks about another person's traits, attitude, or performance reliably generates liking in return, as well as willing compliance with the wishes of the person offering the praise.

Along with cultivating a fruitful relationship, adroit managers can also use praise to repair one that's damaged or unproductive.

Imagine you're the manager of a good-sized unit within your organization. Your work frequently brings you into contact with another manager—call him Dan—whom you have come to dislike. No matter how much you do for him, it's not enough. Worse, he never seems to believe that you're doing the best you can for him. Resenting his attitude and his obvious lack of trust in your abilities and in your good faith, you don't spend as much time with him as you know you should; in consequence, the performance of both his unit and yours is deteriorating.

The research on praise points toward a strategy for fixing the relationship. It may be hard to find, but there has to be something about Dan you can sincerely admire, whether it's his concern for the people in his department, his devotion to his family, or simply his work ethic. In your next encounter with him, make an appreciative comment about that trait. Make it clear that in this case at least, you value what he values. I predict that Dan will relax his relentless negativity and give you an opening to convince him of your competence and good intentions.

The Principle of Reciprocity

People repay in kind.

The application
Give what you want to receive.

Praise is likely to have a warming and softening effect on Dan because, ornery as he is, he is still human and subject to the universal human tendency to treat people the way they treat him. If you have ever caught yourself smiling at a coworker just because he or she smiled first, you know how this principle works.

Charities rely on reciprocity to help them raise funds. For years, for instance, the Disabled American Veterans organization, using only a well-crafted fund-raising letter, garnered a very respectable 18% rate of response to its appeals. But when the group started enclosing a small gift in the envelope, the response rate nearly doubled to 35%. The gift—personalized address labels—was extremely modest, but it wasn't what prospective donors received that made the difference. It was that they had gotten anything at all.

What works in that letter works at the office, too. It's more than an effusion of seasonal spirit, of course, that impels suppliers to shower gifts on purchasing departments at holiday time. In 1996, purchasing managers admitted to an interviewer from *Inc.* magazine that after having accepted a gift from a supplier, they were willing to purchase products and services they would have otherwise declined. Gifts also have a startling effect on retention. I have encouraged readers of my book to send me examples of the principles of influence at work in their own lives. One reader, an employee of the State of Oregon, sent a letter in which she offered these reasons for her commitment to her supervisor:

> He gives me and my son gifts for Christmas and gives me presents on my birthday. There is no promotion for the type of job I have, and my only choice for one is to move to another department. But I find myself resisting trying to move. My boss is reaching retirement age, and I am thinking I will be able to move out after he retires. . . . [F]or now, I feel obligated to stay since he has been so nice to me.

Ultimately, though, gift giving is one of the cruder applications of the rule of reciprocity. In its more sophisticated uses, it confers a genuine first-mover advantage on any manager who is trying to foster positive attitudes and productive personal relationships in the office: Managers can elicit the desired behavior from coworkers and employees by displaying it first. Whether it's a sense of trust, a spirit of cooperation, or a pleasant demeanor, leaders should model the behavior they want to see from others.

The same holds true for managers faced with issues of information delivery and resource allocation. If you lend a member of your staff to a colleague who is shorthanded and staring at a fast-approaching deadline, you will significantly increase your chances of getting help when you need it. Your odds will improve even more if you say, when your colleague thanks you for the assistance, something like, "Sure, glad to help. I know how important it is for me to count on your help when I need it."

The Principle of Social Proof

People follow the lead of similar others.

The application
Use peer power whenever it's available.

Social creatures that they are, human beings rely heavily on the people around them for cues on how to think, feel, and act. We know this intuitively, but intuition has also been confirmed by experiments, such as the one first described in 1982 in the *Journal of Applied Psychology*. A group of researchers went door-to-door in Columbia, South Carolina, soliciting donations for a charity campaign and displaying a list of neighborhood residents who had already donated to the cause. The researchers found that the longer the donor list was, the more likely those solicited would be to donate as well.

To the people being solicited, the friends' and neighbors' names on the list were a form of social evidence about how they should respond. But the evidence would not have been nearly as compelling had the names been those of random strangers. In an experiment from the 1960s, first described in the *Journal of Personality and Social Psychology*, residents of New York City were asked to return a lost wallet to its owner. They were highly likely to attempt to return the wallet when they learned that another New Yorker had previously attempted to do so. But learning that someone from a foreign country had tried to return the wallet didn't sway their decision one way or the other.

The lesson for executives from these two experiments is that persuasion can be extremely effective when it comes from peers. The science supports what most sales professionals already know: Testimonials from satisfied customers work best when the satisfied customer and the prospective customer share similar circumstances. That lesson can help a manager faced with the task of selling a new corporate initiative. Imagine that you're trying to streamline your department's work processes. A group of veteran employees is resisting. Rather than try to convince the employees of the move's merits yourself, ask an old-timer who supports the initiative to speak up for it at a team meeting. The compatriot's testimony stands a much better chance of convincing the group than yet another speech from the boss. Stated simply, influence is often best exerted horizontally rather than vertically.

The Principle of Consistency

People align with their clear commitments.

The application
Make their commitments active, public, and voluntary.

Liking is a powerful force, but the work of persuasion involves more than simply making people feel warmly toward you, your idea, or your product. People need not only to like you but to feel committed to what you want them to do. Good turns are one reliable way to make people feel obligated to you. Another is to win a public commitment from them.

My own research has demonstrated that most people, once they take a stand or go on record in favor of a position, prefer to stick to it. Other studies reinforce that finding and go on to show how even a small, seemingly trivial commitment can have a powerful effect on future actions. Israeli researchers writing in 1983 in the *Personality and Social Psychology Bulletin* recounted how they asked half the residents of a large apartment complex to sign a petition favoring the establishment of a recreation center for the handicapped. The cause was good and the request was small, so almost everyone who was asked agreed to sign. Two weeks later, on National Collection Day for the Handicapped, all residents of the complex were approached at home and asked to give to the cause. A little more than half of those who were not asked to sign the petition made a contribution. But an astounding 92% of those who did sign donated money. The residents of the apartment complex felt obligated to live up to their commitments because those commitments were active, public, and voluntary. These three features are worth considering separately.

There's strong empirical evidence to show that a choice made actively—one that's spoken out loud or written down or otherwise made explicit—is considerably more likely to direct someone's future conduct than the same choice left unspoken. Writing in 1996 in the *Personality and Social Psychology Bulletin*, Delia Cioffi and Randy Garner described an experiment in which college students in one group were asked to fill out a printed form saying they wished to volunteer for an AIDS education project in the public schools. Students in another group volunteered for the same project by leaving blank a form stating that they didn't want to participate. A few days later, when the volunteers reported for duty, 74% of those who showed up were students from the group that signaled their commitment by filling out the form.

The implications are clear for a manager who wants to persuade a subordinate to follow some particular course of action: Get it in writing. Let's suppose you want your employee to submit reports in a more timely fashion. Once you believe you've won agreement, ask him to summarize the decision in a memo and send it to you. By doing so, you'll have greatly increased the odds that he'll fulfill the commitment because, as a rule, people live up to what they have written down.

Research into the social dimensions of commitment suggests that written statements become even more powerful when they're made public. In a classic experiment, described in 1955 in the *Journal of Abnormal and Social Psychology*, college students were asked to estimate the length of lines projected on a screen. Some students were asked to write down their choices on a piece of paper, sign it, and hand the paper to the experimenter. Others wrote their choices on an erasable slate, then erased the slate immediately. Still others were instructed to keep their decisions to themselves.

The experimenters then presented all three groups with evidence that their initial choices may have been wrong. Those who had merely kept their decisions in their heads were the most likely to reconsider their original estimates. More loyal to their first guesses were the students in the group that had written them down and immediately erased them. But by a wide margin, the ones most reluctant to shift from their original choices were those who had signed and handed them to the researcher.

This experiment highlights how much most people wish to appear consistent to others. Consider again the matter of the employee who has been submitting late reports. Recognizing the power of this desire, you should, once you've successfully convinced him of the need to be more timely, reinforce the commitment by making sure it gets a public airing. One way to do that would be to send the employee an email that reads, "I think your plan is just what we need. I showed it to Diane in manufacturing and Phil in shipping, and they thought it was right on target, too." Whatever way such commitments are formalized, they should never be like the New Year's resolutions people privately make and then abandon with no one the wiser. They should be publicly made and visibly posted.

More than 300 years ago, Samuel Butler wrote a couplet that explains succinctly why commitments must be voluntary to be lasting and effective: "He that complies against his will/Is of his own opinion still." If an undertaking is forced, coerced, or imposed from the outside, it's not a commitment; it's an unwelcome burden. Think how you would react if your boss pressured you to donate to the campaign of a political candidate. Would that make you more apt to opt for that candidate in the privacy of a voting booth? Not likely. In fact, in their 1981 book *Psychological Reactance* (Academic Press), Sharon S. Brehm and Jack W. Brehm present data that suggest you'd vote the opposite way just to express your resentment of the boss's coercion.

This kind of backlash can occur in the office, too. Let's return again to that tardy employee. If you want to produce an enduring change in his behavior, you should avoid using threats or pressure tactics to gain his compliance. He'd likely view any change in his

Persuasion Experts, Safe at Last

THANKS TO SEVERAL DECADES OF rigorous empirical research by behavioral scientists, our understanding of the how and why of persuasion has never been broader, deeper, or more detailed. But these scientists aren't the first students of the subject. The history of persuasion studies is an ancient and honorable one, and it has generated a long roster of heroes and martyrs.

A renowned student of social influence, William McGuire, contends in a chapter of the *Handbook of Social Psychology*, 3rd ed. (Oxford University Press, 1985) that scattered among the more than four millennia of recorded Western history are four centuries in which the study of persuasion flourished as a craft. The first was the Periclean Age of ancient Athens, the second occurred during the years of the Roman Republic, the next appeared in the time of the European Renaissance, and the last extended over the hundred years that have just ended, which witnessed the advent of large-scale advertising, information, and mass media campaigns. Each of the three previous centuries of systematic persuasion study was marked by a flowering of human achievement that was suddenly cut short when political authorities had the masters

behavior as the result of intimidation rather than a personal commitment to change. A better approach would be to identify something that the employee genuinely values in the workplace—high-quality workmanship, perhaps, or team spirit—and then describe how timely reports are consistent with those values. That gives the employee reasons for improvement that he can own. And because he owns them, they'll continue to guide his behavior even when you're not watching.

The Principle of Authority

People defer to experts.

The application
Expose your expertise; don't assume it's self-evident.

Two thousand years ago, the Roman poet Virgil offered this simple counsel to those seeking to choose correctly: "Believe an expert." That

of persuasion killed. The philosopher Socrates is probably the best known of the persuasion experts to run afoul of the powers that be.

Information about the persuasion process is a threat because it creates a base of power entirely separate from the one controlled by political authorities. Faced with a rival source of influence, rulers in previous centuries had few qualms about eliminating those rare individuals who truly understood how to marshal forces that heads of state have never been able to monopolize, such as cleverly crafted language, strategically placed information, and, most important, psychological insight.

It would perhaps be expressing too much faith in human nature to claim that persuasion experts no longer face a threat from those who wield political power. But because the truth about persuasion is no longer the sole possession of a few brilliant, inspired individuals, experts in the field can presumably breathe a little easier. Indeed, since most people in power are interested in remaining in power, they're likely to be more interested in acquiring persuasion skills than abolishing them.

may or may not be good advice, but as a description of what people actually do, it can't be beaten. For instance, when the news media present an acknowledged expert's views on a topic, the effect on public opinion is dramatic. A single expert-opinion news story in the *New York Times* is associated with a 2% shift in public opinion nationwide, according to a 1993 study described in the *Public Opinion Quarterly*. And researchers writing in the *American Political Science Review* in 1987 found that when the expert's view was aired on national television, public opinion shifted as much as 4%. A cynic might argue that these findings only illustrate the docile submissiveness of the public. But a fairer explanation is that, amid the teeming complexity of contemporary life, a well-selected expert offers a valuable and efficient shortcut to good decisions. Indeed, some questions, be they legal, financial, medical, or technological, require so much specialized knowledge to answer, we have no choice but to rely on experts.

Since there's good reason to defer to experts, executives should take pains to ensure that they establish their own expertise before they attempt to exert influence. Surprisingly often, people mistakenly assume that others recognize and appreciate their experience. That's what happened at a hospital where some colleagues and I were consulting. The physical therapy staffers were frustrated because so many of their stroke patients abandoned their exercise routines as soon as they left the hospital. No matter how often the staff emphasized the importance of regular home exercise—it is, in fact, crucial to the process of regaining independent function—the message just didn't sink in.

Interviews with some of the patients helped us pinpoint the problem. They were familiar with the background and training of their physicians, but the patients knew little about the credentials of the physical therapists who were urging them to exercise. It was a simple matter to remedy that lack of information: We merely asked the therapy director to display all the awards, diplomas, and certifications of her staff on the walls of the therapy rooms. The result was startling: Exercise compliance jumped 34% and has never dropped since.

What we found immensely gratifying was not just how much we increased compliance, but how. We didn't fool or browbeat any of the patients. We *informed* them into compliance. Nothing had to be invented; no time or resources had to be spent in the process. The staff's expertise was real—all we had to do was make it more visible.

The task for managers who want to establish their claims to expertise is somewhat more difficult. They can't simply nail their diplomas to the wall and wait for everyone to notice. A little subtlety is called for. Outside the United States, it is customary for people to spend time interacting socially before getting down to business for the first time. Frequently they gather for dinner the night before their meeting or negotiation. These get-togethers can make discussions easier and help blunt disagreements—remember the findings about liking and similarity—and they can also provide an opportunity to establish expertise. Perhaps it's a matter of telling an anecdote about successfully solving a problem similar to the one that's on the agenda at the next day's meeting. Or perhaps dinner is the time to describe years spent mastering a complex discipline—not in a boastful way but as part of the ordinary give-and-take of conversation.

Granted, there's not always time for lengthy introductory sessions. But even in the course of the preliminary conversation that precedes most meetings, there is almost always an opportunity to touch lightly on your relevant background and experience as a natural part of a sociable exchange. This initial disclosure of personal information gives you a chance to establish expertise early in the game, so that when the discussion turns to the business at hand, what you have to say will be accorded the respect it deserves.

The Principle of Scarcity

People want more of what they can have less of.

The application

Highlight unique benefits and exclusive information.

Study after study shows that items and opportunities are seen to be more valuable as they become less available. That's a tremendously useful piece of information for managers. They can harness the scarcity principle with the organizational equivalents of limited-time, limited-supply, and one-of-a-kind offers. Honestly informing a coworker of a closing window of opportunity—the chance to get the boss's ear before she leaves for an extended vacation, perhaps—can mobilize action dramatically.

Managers can learn from retailers how to frame their offers not in terms of what people stand to gain but in terms of what they stand to lose if they don't act on the information. The power of "loss language" was demonstrated in a 1988 study of California home owners written up in the *Journal of Applied Psychology*. Half were told that if they fully insulated their homes, they would save a certain amount of money each day. The other half were told that if they failed to insulate, they would lose that amount each day. Significantly more people insulated their homes when exposed to the loss language. The same phenomenon occurs in business. According to a 1994 study in the journal *Organizational Behavior and Human Decision*

Processes, potential losses figure far more heavily in managers' decision making than potential gains.

In framing their offers, executives should also remember that exclusive information is more persuasive than widely available data. A doctoral student of mine, Amram Knishinsky, wrote his 1982 dissertation on the purchase decisions of wholesale beef buyers. He observed that they more than doubled their orders when they were told that, because of certain weather conditions overseas, there was likely to be a scarcity of foreign beef in the near future. But their orders increased 600% when they were informed that no one else had that information yet.

The persuasive power of exclusivity can be harnessed by any manager who comes into possession of information that's not broadly available and that supports an idea or initiative he or she would like the organization to adopt. The next time that kind of information crosses your desk, round up your organization's key players. The information itself may seem dull, but exclusivity will give it a special sheen. Push it across your desk and say, "I just got this report today. It won't be distributed until next week, but I want to give you an early look at what it shows." Then watch your listeners lean forward.

Allow me to stress here a point that should be obvious. No offer of exclusive information, no exhortation to act now or miss this opportunity forever should be made unless it is genuine. Deceiving colleagues into compliance is not only ethically objectionable, it's foolhardy. If the deception is detected—and it certainly will be—it will snuff out any enthusiasm the offer originally kindled. It will also invite dishonesty toward the deceiver. Remember the rule of reciprocity.

Putting It All Together

There's nothing abstruse or obscure about these six principles of persuasion. Indeed, they neatly codify our intuitive understanding of the ways people evaluate information and form decisions. As a result, the principles are easy for most people to grasp, even those with no formal education in psychology. But in the seminars and workshops I conduct, I have learned that two points bear repeated emphasis.

First, although the six principles and their applications can be discussed separately for the sake of clarity, they should be applied in combination to compound their impact. For instance, in discussing the importance of expertise, I suggested that managers use informal, social conversations to establish their credentials. But that conversation affords an opportunity to gain information as well as convey it. While you're showing your dinner companion that you have the skills and experience your business problem demands, you can also learn about your companion's background, likes, and dislikes—information that will help you locate genuine similarities and give sincere compliments. By letting your expertise surface and also establishing rapport, you double your persuasive power. And if you succeed in bringing your dinner partner on board, you may encourage other people to sign on as well, thanks to the persuasive power of social evidence.

The other point I wish to emphasize is that the rules of ethics apply to the science of social influence just as they do to any other technology. Not only is it ethically wrong to trick or trap others into assent, it's ill-advised in practical terms. Dishonest or high-pressure tactics work only in the short run, if at all. Their long-term effects are malignant, especially within an organization, which can't function properly without a bedrock level of trust and cooperation.

That point is made vividly in the following account, which a department head for a large textile manufacturer related at a training workshop I conducted. She described a vice president in her company who wrung public commitments from department heads in a highly manipulative manner. Instead of giving his subordinates time to talk or think through his proposals carefully, he would approach them individually at the busiest moment of their workday and describe the benefits of his plan in exhaustive, patience-straining detail. Then he would move in for the kill. "It's very important for me to see you as being on my team on this," he would say. "Can I count on your support?" Intimidated, frazzled, eager to chase the man from their offices so they could get back to work, the department heads would invariably go along with his request. But because the commitments never felt voluntary, the department heads never followed through, and as a result the vice president's initiatives all blew up or petered out.

This story had a deep impact on the other participants in the workshop. Some gulped in shock as they recognized their own manipulative behavior. But what stopped everyone cold was the expression on the department head's face as she recounted the damaging collapse of her superior's proposals. She was smiling.

Nothing I could say would more effectively make the point that the deceptive or coercive use of the principles of social influence is ethically wrong and pragmatically wrongheaded. Yet the same principles, if applied appropriately, can steer decisions correctly. Legitimate expertise, genuine obligations, authentic similarities, real social proof, exclusive news, and freely made commitments can produce choices that are likely to benefit both parties. And any approach that works to everyone's mutual benefit is good business, don't you think? Of course, I don't want to press you into it, but, if you agree, I would love it if you could just jot me a memo to that effect.

Originally published in September 2001. Reprint RO109D

How to Give a Killer Presentation

by Chris Anderson

A LITTLE MORE THAN A YEAR AGO, on a trip to Nairobi, Kenya, some colleagues and I met a 12-year-old Masai boy named Richard Turere, who told us a fascinating story. His family raises livestock on the edge of a vast national park, and one of the biggest challenges is protecting the animals from lions—especially at night. Richard had noticed that placing lamps in a field didn't deter lion attacks, but when he walked the field with a torch, the lions stayed away. From a young age, he'd been interested in electronics, teaching himself by, for example, taking apart his parents' radio. He used that experience to devise a system of lights that would turn on and off in sequence—using solar panels, a car battery, and a motorcycle indicator box—and thereby create a sense of movement that he hoped would scare off the lions. He installed the lights, and the lions stopped attacking. Soon villages elsewhere in Kenya began installing Richard's "lion lights."

The story was inspiring and worthy of the broader audience that our TED conference could offer, but on the surface, Richard seemed an unlikely candidate to give a TED Talk. He was painfully shy. His English was halting. When he tried to describe his invention, the sentences tumbled out incoherently. And frankly, it was hard to imagine a preteenager standing on a stage in front of 1,400 people accustomed to hearing from polished speakers such as Bill Gates, Sir Ken Robinson, and Jill Bolte Taylor.

But Richard's story was so compelling that we invited him to speak. In the months before the 2013 conference, we worked with him to frame his story—to find the right place to begin, and to develop a succinct and logical arc of events. On the back of his invention Richard had won a scholarship to one of Kenya's best schools, and there he had the chance to practice the talk several times in front of a live audience. It was critical that he build his confidence to the point where his personality could shine through. When he finally gave his talk at TED, in Long Beach, you could tell he was nervous, but that only made him more engaging—people were hanging on his every word. The confidence was there, and every time Richard smiled, the audience melted. When he finished, the response was instantaneous: a sustained standing ovation.

Since the first TED conference, 30 years ago, speakers have run the gamut from political figures, musicians, and TV personalities who are completely at ease before a crowd to lesser-known academics, scientists, and writers—some of whom feel deeply uncomfortable giving presentations. Over the years, we've sought to develop a process for helping inexperienced presenters to frame, practice, and deliver talks that people enjoy watching. It typically begins six to nine months before the event, and involves cycles of devising (and revising) a script, repeated rehearsals, and plenty of fine-tuning. We're continually tweaking our approach—because the art of public speaking is evolving in real time—but judging by public response, our basic regimen works well: Since we began putting TED Talks online, in 2006, they've been viewed more than one billion times.

On the basis of this experience, I'm convinced that giving a good talk is highly coachable. In a matter of hours, a speaker's content and delivery can be transformed from muddled to mesmerizing. And while my team's experience has focused on TED's 18-minutes-or-shorter format, the lessons we've learned are surely useful to other presenters—whether it's a CEO doing an IPO road show, a brand manager unveiling a new product, or a start-up pitching to VCs.

Idea in Brief

There are five keys to giving a great presentation:

- Frame your story (figure out where to start and where to end).

- Plan your delivery (decide whether to memorize your speech word for word or develop bullet points and then rehearse it—over and over).

- Work on stage presence (but remember that your story matters more than how you stand or whether you're visibly nervous).

- Plan the multimedia (whatever you do, don't read from Power-Point slides).

- Put it together (play to your strengths and be authentic).

Presentations rise or fall on the quality of the idea, the narrative, and the passion of the speaker. It's about substance—not style. In fact, it's fairly easy to "coach out" the problems in a talk, but there's no way to "coach in" the basic story—the presenter has to have the raw material. So if your thinking is not there yet, decline that invitation to speak. Instead, keep working until you have an idea that's worth sharing.

Frame Your Story

There's no way you can give a good talk unless you have something worth talking about. Conceptualizing and framing what you want to say is the most vital part of preparation.

We all know that humans are wired to listen to stories, and metaphors abound for the narrative structures that work best to engage people. When I think about compelling presentations, I think about taking an audience on a journey. A successful talk is a little miracle—people see the world differently afterward.

If you frame the talk as a journey, the biggest decisions are figuring out where to start and where to end. To find the right place to start, consider what people in the audience already know about your subject—and how much they care about it. If you assume they have more knowledge or interest than they do, or if you start using jargon or get too technical, you'll lose them. The most engaging speakers do a superb job of very quickly introducing the topic, explaining why they care so deeply about it, and convincing the audience members that they should, too.

The biggest problem I see in first drafts of presentations is that they try to cover too much ground. You can't summarize an entire career in a single talk. If you try to cram in everything you know, you won't have time to include key details, and your talk will disappear into abstract language that may make sense if your listeners are familiar with the subject matter but will be completely opaque if they're new to it. You need specific examples to flesh out your ideas. So limit the scope of your talk to that which can be explained, and brought to life with examples, in the available time. Much of the early feedback we give aims to correct the impulse to sweep too broadly. Instead, go deeper. Give more detail. Don't tell us about your entire field of study—tell us about your unique contribution.

Of course, it can be just as damaging to overexplain or painstakingly draw out the implications of a talk. And there the remedy is different: Remember that the people in the audience are intelligent. Let them figure some things out for themselves. Let them draw their own conclusions.

Many of the best talks have a narrative structure that loosely follows a detective story. The speaker starts out by presenting a problem and then describes the search for a solution. There's an "aha" moment, and the audience's perspective shifts in a meaningful way.

If a talk fails, it's almost always because the speaker didn't frame it correctly, misjudged the audience's level of interest, or neglected to tell a story. Even if the topic is important, random pontification without narrative is always deeply unsatisfying. There's no progression, and you don't feel that you're learning.

I was at an energy conference recently where two people—a city mayor and a former governor—gave back-to-back talks. The mayor's talk was essentially a list of impressive projects his city had undertaken. It came off as boasting, like a report card or an advertisement for his reelection. It quickly got boring. When the governor spoke, she didn't list achievements; instead, she shared an idea. Yes, she recounted anecdotes from her time in office, but the idea was

Find the Perfect Mix of Data and Narrative

by Nancy Duarte

MOST PRESENTATIONS LIE SOMEWHERE on the continuum between a report and a story. A report is data-rich, exhaustive, and informative—but not very engaging. Stories help a speaker connect with an audience, but listeners often want facts and information, too. Great presenters layer story and information like a cake, and understand that different types of talks require differing ingredients.

Report
Literal,
informational,
factual,
exhaustive

Story
Dramatic,
experiential,
evocative,
persuasive

Research findings	Financial presentation	Product launch	VC pitch	Keynote address
If your goal is to communicate information from a written report, send the full document to the audience in advance, and limit the presentation to key takeaways. Don't do a long slide show that repeats all your findings. Anyone who's really interested can read the report; everyone else will appreciate brevity.	Financial audiences love data, and they'll want the details. Satisfy their analytical appetite with facts, but add a thread of narrative to appeal to their emotional side. Then present the key takeaways visually, to help them find meaning in the numbers.	Instead of covering only specs and features, focus on the value your product brings to the world. Tell stories that show how real people will use it and why it will change their lives.	For 30 minutes with a VC, prepare a crisp, well-structured story arc that conveys your idea compellingly in 10 minutes or less; then let Q&A drive the rest of the meeting. Anticipate questions and rehearse clear and concise answers.	Formal talks at big events are high-stakes, high-impact opportunities to take your listeners on a transformative journey. Use a clear story framework and aim to engage them emotionally.

central—and the stories explanatory or illustrative (and also funny). It was so much more interesting. The mayor's underlying point seemed to be how great he was, while the governor's message was "Here's a compelling idea that would benefit us all."

As a general rule, people are not very interested in talks about organizations or institutions (unless they're members of them). Ideas and stories fascinate us; organizations bore us—they're much harder to relate to. (Businesspeople especially take note: Don't boast about your company; rather, tell us about the problem you're solving.)

Plan Your Delivery

Once you've got the framing down, it's time to focus on your delivery. There are three main ways to deliver a talk. You can read it directly off a script or a teleprompter. You can develop a set of bullet points that map out what you're going to say in each section rather than scripting the whole thing word for word. Or you can memorize your talk, which entails rehearsing it to the point where you internalize every word—verbatim.

My advice: Don't read it, and don't use a teleprompter. It's usually just too distancing—people will know you're reading. And as soon as they sense it, the way they receive your talk will shift. Suddenly your intimate connection evaporates, and everything feels a lot more formal. We generally outlaw reading approaches of any kind at TED, though we made an exception a few years ago for a man who insisted on using a monitor. We set up a screen at the back of the auditorium, in the hope that the audience wouldn't notice it. At first he spoke naturally. But soon he stiffened up, and you could see this horrible sinking feeling pass through the audience as people realized, "Oh, no, he's reading to us!" The words were great, but the talk got poor ratings.

Many of our best and most popular TED Talks have been memorized word for word. If you're giving an important talk and you have the time to do this, it's the best way to go. But don't underestimate the work involved. One of our most memorable speakers was Jill Bolte Taylor, a brain researcher who had suffered a stroke. She talked about what she learned during the eight years it took her to recover. After crafting her story and undertaking many hours of solo practice, she rehearsed her talk dozens of times in front of an audience to be sure she had it down.

Obviously, not every presentation is worth that kind of investment of time. But if you do decide to memorize your talk, be aware that there's a predictable arc to the learning curve. Most people go through what I call the "valley of awkwardness," where they haven't quite memorized the talk. If they give the talk while stuck in that valley, the audience will sense it. Their words will sound recited, or there will be painful moments where they stare into the middle distance, or cast their eyes upward, as they struggle to remember their lines. This creates distance between the speaker and the audience.

Getting past this point is simple, fortunately. It's just a matter of rehearsing enough times that the flow of words becomes second nature. Then you can focus on delivering the talk with meaning and authenticity. Don't worry—you'll get there.

But if you don't have time to learn a speech thoroughly and get past that awkward valley, don't try. Go with bullet points on note cards. As long as you know what you want to say for each one, you'll be fine. Focus on remembering the transitions from one bullet point to the next.

Also pay attention to your tone. Some speakers may want to come across as authoritative or wise or powerful or passionate, but it's usually much better to just sound conversational. Don't force it. Don't orate. Just be you.

If a successful talk is a journey, make sure you don't start to annoy your travel companions along the way. Some speakers project too much ego. They sound condescending or full of themselves, and the audience shuts down. Don't let that happen.

Develop Stage Presence

For inexperienced speakers, the physical act of being onstage can be the most difficult part of giving a presentation—but people tend to overestimate its importance. Getting the words, story, and substance right is a much bigger determinant of success or failure than how

How to Stop Saying "Um," "Ah," and "You Know"

by Noah Zandan

Um.

Ah.

So.

You know.

Like.

Right?

Well.

WHEN WE FIND OURSELVES RATTLED while speaking—whether we're nervous, distracted, or at a loss for what comes next—it's easy to lean on filler words. These may give us a moment to collect our thoughts before we press on, and in some cases, they may be useful indicators that the audience should pay special attention to what we're about to say. But when we start to overuse them, they become verbal crutches that diminish our credibility and distract from our message.

The good news is that you can turn this weakness into a strength by replacing filler words with pauses.

Research suggests that most conversational speech consists of short (0.20 second), medium (0.60 second), and long (over 1 second) pauses. Great public speakers often pause for two to three seconds or even longer. My firm's phonetic data shows that the average speaker uses only 3.5 pauses per minute, and that's not enough.

you stand or whether you're visibly nervous. And when it comes to stage presence, a little coaching can go a long way.

The biggest mistake we see in early rehearsals is that people move their bodies too much. They sway from side to side, or shift their weight from one leg to the other. People do this naturally when they're nervous, but it's distracting and makes the speaker seem weak. Simply getting a person to keep his or her lower body motionless can dramatically improve stage presence. There are some people

This is understandable. For many speakers, even the briefest pause can feel like an interminable silence. That's because we tend to think faster than we speak.

Despite how they might feel at first, well-placed pauses make you sound calm and collected, and they help you gather your thoughts, calm your nerves, and build suspense.

The first step in changing any habit is awareness. To identify your crutch words, watch the video or review the transcript of your most recent talk, and determine what vocal fillers you rely on most. Once you're aware of them, you'll likely start to hear yourself say these words in your day-to-day communication. Pair your crutch words with actions. So for instance, every time you catch yourself saying "like," tap your leg. Or have a family member or close friend monitor a practice session and bring your attention to your crutch words with a clap or a finger snap.

Next, begin forcing yourself to be silent. To practice, record yourself on video talking about what you did from the beginning to the end of the day. Rehearse using pauses instead of filler words as you recall the events.

Finally, I can't stress enough the importance of preparation. Nervousness is one of the biggest reasons people overuse vocal fillers. The less prepared you are, the more nervous you'll be, which will likely cause you to speak too quickly, trip over your words, or forget what's next. So practice. On average, the optimal ratio of preparation to performance is one hour of practice for every minute of performance. This might sound like a lot, but Trey Guinn, a professor of communications at the University of Texas at Austin, recommends speakers get in at least three trial runs before stepping in front of an audience.

who are able to walk around a stage during a presentation, and that's fine if it comes naturally. But the vast majority are better off standing still and relying on hand gestures for emphasis.

Perhaps the most important physical act onstage is making eye contact. Find five or six friendly looking people in different parts of the audience and look them in the eye as you speak. Think of them as friends you haven't seen in a year, whom you're bringing up to date on your work. That eye contact is incredibly powerful, and it will do more than anything else to help your talk land. Even if you don't have time to prepare fully and have to read from a script, looking up and making eye contact will make a huge difference.

Another big hurdle for inexperienced speakers is nervousness—both in advance of the talk and while they're onstage. People deal with this in different ways. Many speakers stay out in the audience until the moment they go on; this can work well, because keeping your mind engaged in the earlier speakers can distract you and limit nervousness. Amy Cuddy, a Harvard Business School professor who studies how certain body poses can affect power, utilized one of the more unusual preparation techniques I've seen. She recommends that people spend time before a talk striding around, standing tall, and extending their bodies; these poses make you feel more powerful. It's what she did before going onstage, and she delivered a phenomenal talk. But I think the single best advice is simply to breathe deeply before you go onstage. It works.

In general, people worry too much about nervousness. Nerves are not a disaster. The audience *expects* you to be nervous. It's a natural body response that can actually improve your performance: It gives you energy to perform and keeps your mind sharp. Just keep breathing, and you'll be fine.

Acknowledging nervousness can also create engagement. Showing your vulnerability, whether through nerves or tone of voice, is one of the most powerful ways to win over an audience, provided it is authentic. Susan Cain, who wrote a book about introverts and spoke at our 2012 conference, was terrified about giving her talk. You could feel her fragility onstage, and it created this dynamic where the audience was rooting for her—everybody wanted to hug her afterward. The fact that we knew she was fighting to keep herself up there made it beautiful, and it was the most popular talk that year.

Plan the Multimedia

With so much technology at our disposal, it may feel almost mandatory to use, at a minimum, presentation slides. By now most people have heard the advice about PowerPoint: Keep it simple; don't use a slide deck as a substitute for notes (by, say, listing the bullet points you'll discuss—those are best put on note cards); and don't repeat out loud words that are on the slide. Not only is reciting slides a variation of the teleprompter problem—"Oh, no, she's reading to us, too!"—but information is interesting only once, and hearing and seeing the same words feels repetitive. That advice may seem universal by now, but go into any company and you'll see presenters violating it every day.

Many of the best TED speakers don't use slides at all, and many talks don't require them. If you have photographs or illustrations that make the topic come alive, then yes, show them. If not, consider doing without, at least for some parts of the presentation. And if you're going to use slides, it's worth exploring alternatives to PowerPoint. For instance, TED has invested in the company Prezi, which makes presentation software that offers a camera's-eye view of a two-dimensional landscape. Instead of a flat sequence of images, you can move around the landscape and zoom in to it if need be. Used properly, such techniques can dramatically boost the visual punch of a talk and enhance its meaning.

Artists, architects, photographers, and designers have the best opportunity to use visuals. Slides can help frame and pace a talk and help speakers avoid getting lost in jargon or overly intellectual language. (Art can be hard to talk about—better to experience it visually.) I've seen great presentations in which the artist or designer put slides on an automatic timer so that the image changed every 15 seconds. I've also seen presenters give a talk accompanied by video, speaking along to it. That can help sustain momentum. The industrial designer Ross Lovegrove's highly visual TED Talk, for instance, used this technique to bring the audience along on a remarkable creative journey.

Another approach creative types might consider is to build silence into their talks, and just let the work speak for itself. The kinetic sculptor Reuben Margolin used that approach to powerful effect. The idea is not to think "I'm giving a talk." Instead, think "I want to give this audience a powerful experience of my work." The single worst thing artists and architects can do is to retreat into abstract or conceptual language.

Video has obvious uses for many speakers. In a TED Talk about the intelligence of crows, for instance, the scientist showed a clip of a crow bending a hook to fish a piece of food out of a tube—essentially creating a tool. It illustrated his point far better than anything he could have said.

Used well, video can be very effective, but there are common mistakes that should be avoided. A clip needs to be short—if it's more than 60 seconds, you risk losing people. Don't use videos—particularly corporate ones—that sound self-promotional or like infomercials; people are conditioned to tune those out. Anything with a soundtrack can be dangerously off-putting. And whatever you do, don't show a clip of yourself being interviewed on, say, CNN. I've seen speakers do this, and it's a really bad idea—no one wants to go along with you on your ego trip. The people in your audience are already listening to you live; why would they want to simultaneously watch your talking-head clip on a screen?

Putting It Together

We start helping speakers prepare their talks six months (or more) in advance so that they'll have plenty of time to practice. We want people's talks to be in final form at least a month before the event. The more practice they can do in the final weeks, the better off they'll be. Ideally, they'll practice the talk on their own and in front of an audience.

The tricky part about rehearsing a presentation in front of other people is that they will feel obligated to offer feedback and constructive criticism. Often the feedback from different people will vary or directly conflict. This can be confusing or even paralyzing, which is why it's important to be choosy about the people you use as a test audience, and whom you invite to offer feedback. In general, the more experience a person has as a presenter, the better the criticism he or she can offer.

I learned many of these lessons myself in 2011. My colleague Bruno Giussani, who curates our TEDGlobal event, pointed out that although I'd worked at TED for nine years, served as the emcee at our

10 Ways to Ruin a Presentation

AS HARD AS IT MAY BE to give a great talk, it's really easy to blow it. Here are some common mistakes that TED advises its speakers to avoid.

1. Take a really long time to explain what your talk is about.

2. Speak slowly and dramatically. Why talk when you can orate?

3. Make sure you subtly let everyone know how important you are.

4. Refer to your book repeatedly. Even better, quote yourself from it.

5. Cram your slides with numerous text bullet points and multiple fonts.

6. Use lots of unexplained technical jargon to make yourself sound smart.

7. Speak at great length about the history of your organization and its glorious achievements.

8. Don't bother rehearsing to check how long your talk is running.

9. Sound as if you're reciting your talk from memory.

10. Never, ever make eye contact with anyone in the audience.

conferences, and introduced many of the speakers, I'd never actually given a TED Talk myself. So he invited me to give one, and I accepted.

It was more stressful than I'd expected. Even though I spend time helping others frame their stories, framing my own in a way that felt compelling was difficult. I decided to memorize my presentation, which was about how web video powers global innovation, and that was really hard: Even though I was putting in a lot of hours, and getting sound advice from my colleagues, I definitely hit a point where I didn't quite have it down and began to doubt I ever would. I really thought I might bomb. I was nervous right up until the moment I took the stage. But it ended up going fine. It's definitely not one of the all-time great TED Talks, but it got a positive reaction—and I survived the stress of going through it.

Ultimately I learned firsthand what our speakers have been discovering for three decades: Presentations rise or fall on the quality of the idea, the narrative, and the passion of the speaker. It's about substance, not speaking style or multimedia pyrotechnics. It's fairly easy to "coach out" the problems in a talk, but there's no way to "coach in" the basic story—the presenter has to have the raw material. If you have something to say, you can build a great talk. But if the central theme isn't there, you're better off not speaking. Decline the invitation. Go back to work, and wait until you have a compelling idea that's really worth sharing.

The single most important thing to remember is that there is no one good way to do a talk. The most memorable talks offer something fresh, something no one has seen before. The worst ones are those that feel formulaic. So do not on any account try to emulate every piece of advice I've offered here. Take the bulk of it on board, sure. But make the talk your own. You know what's distinctive about you and your idea. Play to your strengths and give a talk that is truly authentic to you.

Originally published in June 2013. Reprint R1306K

The Science of Strong Business Writing

Lessons from neurobiology.

by Bill Birchard

STRONG WRITING SKILLS are essential for anyone in business. You need them to effectively communicate with colleagues, employees, and bosses and to sell any ideas, products, or services you're offering.

Many people, especially in the corporate world, think good writing is an art—and that those who do it well have an innate talent they've nurtured through experience, intuition, and a habit of reading often and widely. But every day we're learning more about the science of good writing. Advances in neurobiology and psychology show, with data and in images, exactly how the brain responds to words, phrases, and stories. And the criteria for making better writing choices are more objective than you might think.

Good writing gets the reader's dopamine flowing in the area of the brain known as the reward circuit. Great writing releases opioids that turn on reward hot spots. Just like good food, a soothing bath, or an enveloping hug, well-executed prose makes us feel pleasure, which makes us want to keep reading.

Most of the rules you learned in school—"Show, don't tell" or "Use the active voice"—still hold. But the reasons they do are now clearer. Scientists using MRI and PET machines can literally see how reward regions clustered in the midbrain light up when people read certain types of writing or hear it spoken aloud. Each word, phrase, or idea acts as a stimulus, causing the brain to instantly answer a stream of questions: Does this promise value? Will I like it? Can I learn from it?

Kent Berridge, a pioneering University of Michigan psychologist and neuroscientist, notes that researchers originally believed that the reward circuit largely handled sensory cues. But, he explains, "it's become clear in the past 50 years from neuroimaging studies that all kinds of social and cultural rewards can also activate this system."

Whether it's a succinct declarative statement in an email or a complex argument in a report, your own writing has the potential to light up the neural circuitry of your readers' brains. (The same is true if you read the words to an audience.) The magic happens when prose has one or more of these characteristics: It's simple, specific, surprising, stirring, seductive, smart, social, or story-driven. In my work as an author and a writing coach for businesspeople, I've found those eight S's to be hallmarks of the best writing. And scientific evidence backs up their power.

Simplicity

"Keep it simple." This classic piece of writing advice stands on the most basic neuroscience research. Simplicity increases what scientists call the brain's "processing fluency." Short sentences, familiar words, and clean syntax ensure that the reader doesn't have to exert too much brainpower to understand your meaning.

By contrast, studies have shown that sentences with clauses nested in the middle take longer to read and cause more comprehension mistakes. Ditto for most sentences in the passive voice. If you write "Profits are loved by investors," for example, instead of "Investors love profits," you're switching the standard positions of the verb and the direct object. That can cut comprehension accuracy by 10% and take a tenth of a second longer to read.

Idea in Brief

The Research

Brain scans are showing us in new detail exactly what entices readers. Scientists can see a group of midbrain neurons—the "reward circuit"—light up as people respond to everything from a simple metaphor to an unexpected story twist. The big takeaway? Whether you're crafting an email to a colleague or an important report for the board, you can write in a way that delights readers on a primal level, releasing pleasure chemicals in their brains.

How to Do It

There are eight features of satisfying writing: simplicity, specificity, surprise, stirring language, seductiveness, smart ideas, social content, and storytelling. They're effective tools for engaging readers because they trigger the same neural responses that other pleasurable stimuli do. Learning how to use these eight S's can captivate readers and help your message stick.

Tsuyoshi Okuhara, of the University of Tokyo, teamed with colleagues to ask 400 people aged 40 to 69 to read about how to exercise for better health. Half the group got long-winded, somewhat technical material. The other half got an easy-to-read edit of the same content. The group reading the simple version—with shorter words and sentences, among other things—scored higher on self-efficacy: They expressed more confidence in succeeding.

Even more noteworthy: Humans learn from experience that simpler explanations are not always right, but they *usually* are. Andrey Kolmogorov, a Russian mathematician, proved decades ago that people infer that simpler patterns yield better predictions, explanations, and decisions. That means you're more persuasive when you reduce overdressed ideas to their naked state.

Cutting extraneous words and using the active voice are two ways to keep it simple. Another tactic is to drill down to what's really salient and scrap tangential details. Let's say you have researched crossover markets and are recommending options in a memo to senior leaders. Instead of sharing every pro and con for each market—that is, taking the exhaustive approach—maybe pitch just the top two prospects and identify their principal pluses and minuses.

Specificity

Specifics awaken a swath of brain circuits. Think of "pelican" versus "bird." Or "wipe" versus "clean." In one study, the more-specific words in those pairs activated more neurons in the visual and motor-strip parts of the brain than did the general ones, which means they caused the brain to process meaning more robustly.

Years ago scientists thought our brains decoded words as symbols. Now we understand that our neurons actually "embody" what the words mean: When we hear more-specific ones, we "taste," "feel," and "see" traces of the real thing.

Remarkably, the simulation may extend to our muscles too. When a team led by an Italian researcher, Marco Tettamanti, asked people to listen to sentences related to the mouth, hand, and leg—"I bite an apple"; "I grasp a knife"; "I kick the ball"—the brain regions for moving their jaws, hands, and legs fired.

Using more-vivid, palpable language will reward your readers. In a recent letter to shareholders, Amazon CEO Jeff Bezos didn't say, "We're facing strong competition." Channeling Tettamanti's research, he wrote, "Third-party sellers are kicking our first-party butt. Badly."

Another specificity tactic is to give readers a memorable shorthand phrase to help them retain your message. Malcolm Gladwell coined "the tipping point." Management gurus W. Chan Kim and Renée Mauborgne came up with "blue ocean strategy"; essayist Nassim Nicholas Taleb, "black swan event."

Surprise

Our brains are wired to make nonstop predictions, including guessing the next word in every line of text. If your writing confirms the readers' guess, that's OK, though possibly a yawner. Surprise can make your message stick, helping readers learn and retain information.

Jean-Louis Dessalles, a researcher in artificial intelligence and cognitive science at Télécom Paris, conducted an experiment that demonstrated people's affinity for the unexpected. He asked participants to read short, unfinished narratives and consider different possible endings for each. For example, one story read: "Two weeks after my car had been stolen, the police informed me that a car that might be mine was for sale on the internet . . . . The phone number had been identified. It was the mobile phone number of . . . ." The choices were (a) "my office colleague," (b) "a colleague of my brother's," or (c) "someone in my neighborhood." For 17 of 18 stories, the vast majority of people preferred the most unexpected ending (in this example, the work colleague). They didn't want a story that fulfilled their predictions.

So reward your readers with novelty. Jonah Berger and Katherine Milkman, of the Wharton School, saw the impact of surprising content when they examined nearly 7,000 articles that appeared online in the *New York Times*. They found that those rated as surprising were 14% more likely to be on the newspaper's "most-emailed" list.

Readers appreciate unusual wordplay, too. A good example is John McPhee's characterization of World War II as a "technological piñata." Or consider how a Texas-based conglomerate described itself in its 2016 shareholder letter: "Think of Biglari Holdings as a museum of businesses. Our preference is to collect masterpieces."

Stirring Language

You may think you're more likely to persuade with logic, but no. Our brains process the emotional connotations of a word within 200 milliseconds of reading it—much faster than we understand its meaning. So when we read emotionally charged material, we reflexively react with feelings—fear, joy, awe, disgust, and so forth—because our brains have been trained since hunter-gatherer times to respond that way. Reason follows. We then combine the immediate feeling and subsequent thought to create meaning.

How sensitive are we to emotion? Experiments show that when people hear a list of words, they often miss a few as a result of "attentional blinks" caused by limits in our brain processing power. But we don't miss the emotionally significant words. With those there are no blinks.

So when you write your next memo, consider injecting words that package feeling and thought together. Instead of saying "challenge the competition," you might use "outwit rivals." In lieu of "promote innovation," try "prize ingenuity." Metaphor often works even better. Canadian researchers Andrea Bowes and Albert Katz tested relatively bland phrases like "What a very good idea!" and "Be careful what you say" against more-evocative expressions like "What a gem of an idea!" and "Watch your back." Readers reacted more strongly to the latter.

Just a small touch can drive the neural circuits for emotion. So before you start composing, get your feelings straight, along with your facts. Zeal for your message will show through. And if you express your emotion, readers will feel it.

Seductiveness

As humans, we're wired to savor anticipation. One famous study showed that people are often happier planning a vacation than they are after taking one. Scientists call the reward "anticipatory utility." You can build up the same sort of excitement when you structure your writing. In experiments using poetry, researchers found that readers' reward circuitry reached peak firing several seconds before the high points of emphatic lines and stanzas. Brain images show preemptive spikes of pleasure even in readers with no previous interest in poetry.

You can generate a similar reaction by winding up people's curiosity for what's to come. Steve Jobs did this in his famous "How to Live Before You Die" commencement address to Stanford University's class of 2005. "I never graduated from college," he began. "Truth be told, this is the closest I've ever gotten to a college graduation. Today I want to tell you three stories from my life. That's it. No big deal. Just three stories." Are you on the edge of your seat to hear what the three stories are?

So start a report with a question. Pose your customer problem as a conundrum. Position your product development work as solving a mystery. Put readers in a state of uncertainty so that you can then lead them to something better.

Smart Thinking

Making people feel smart—giving them an "aha" moment—is another way to please readers. To show how these sudden "pops" of insight activate the brain, researchers have asked people to read three words (for example, "house," "bark," and "apple") and then identify a fourth word that relates to all three, while MRI machines and EEGs record their brain activity. When the study participants arrive at a solution ("tree"), brain regions near the right temple light up, and so do parts of the reward circuit in the prefrontal cortex and midbrain. The readers' delight is visible. Psychological research also reveals how people feel after such moments: at ease, certain, and—most of all—happy.

How can you write to create an aha moment for your readers? One way is to draw fresh distinctions. Ginni Rometty, formerly IBM's CEO, offered one with this description of the future: "It will not be a world of man versus machine; it will be a world of man plus machine."

Another strategy is to phrase a pragmatic message so that it also evokes a perennial, universal truth. The late Max De Pree, founder and CEO of the office furniture company Herman Miller, had a knack for speaking to employees this way. In *Leadership Is an Art* he wrote: "The first responsibility of a leader is to define reality. The last is to say thank you. In between the two, the leader must become a servant and a debtor." That's wisdom not just for business managers but for parents, teachers, coaches—anyone in a guiding role.

Social Content

Our brains are wired to crave human connection—even in what we read. Consider a study of readers' responses to different kinds of literary excerpts: some with vivid descriptions of people or their thoughts, and others without such a focus. The passages that included people activated the areas of participants' brains that interpret social signals, which in turn triggered their reward circuits.

We don't want just to read about people, though—we want to understand what they're thinking as quickly as possible. A study led by Frank Van Overwalle, a social neuroscientist at Vrije Universiteit Brussel, found that readers infer the goals of people they're reading about in under 350 milliseconds, and discern their character traits within 650 milliseconds.

One way to help readers connect with you and your writing is to reveal more traces of yourself in it. Think voice, worldview, vocabulary, wit, syntax, poetic rhythm, sensibilities. Take the folksy—and effective—speeches and letters of Berkshire Hathaway CEO Warren Buffett. His bon mots include "Someone's sitting in the shade today because someone planted a tree a long time ago," "It's only when the tide goes out that you discover who's been swimming naked," and "Beware of geeks bearing formulas."

Remember also to include the human angle in any topic you're discussing. When you want to make a point about a supply-chain hiccup, for example, don't frame the problem as a "trucking disconnect." Write instead about mixed signals between the driver and dispatcher.

Another simple trick to engage readers is to use the second person ("you"), as I've done throughout this piece. This can be particularly helpful when you're explaining technical or complicated material. For example, psychologist Richard Mayer and colleagues at the University of California, Santa Barbara, ran experiments with two versions of an online presentation on the respiratory system. Each included 100 words of spoken text paired with simple animations. But one version used the impersonal third person ("During inhaling, *the* diaphragm moves down, creating more space for *the* lungs . . ."), while the other was more personal ("*your* diaphragm" and "*your* lungs"). People who listened to the latter scored significantly higher than their counterparts on a test that measured what they had learned.

Storytelling

Few things beat a good anecdote. Stories, even fragments of them, captivate extensive portions of readers' brains in part because they combine many of the elements I've described already.

Research by Uri Hasson at Princeton reveals the neural effect of an engaging tale. Functional MRI scans show that when a story begins, listeners' brains immediately begin glowing in a specific pattern. What's more, that grid reflects the storyteller's exactly. Other research shows that, at the same time, midbrain regions of the reward circuit come to life.

Experiments by behavioral scientists at the University of Florida produced similar results. Brain images showed heightened activity in reward regions among people who read 12-second narratives that prompted pleasant images. (A sample narrative: "It's the last few minutes of the big game and it's close. The crowd explodes in a deafening roar. You jump up, cheering. Your team has come from behind to win.")

When you incorporate stories into your communications, big payoffs can result. Consider research that Melissa Lynne Murphy did at the University of Texas, looking at business crowdfunding campaigns. She found that study participants formed more-favorable impressions of the pitches that had richer narratives, giving them higher marks for entrepreneur credibility and business legitimacy. Study participants also expressed more willingness to invest in the projects and share information about them. The implication: No stories, no great funding success.

The eight s's can be your secret weapons in writing well. They're effective tools for engaging readers because they trigger the same neural responses that other pleasurable stimuli do. And you probably understand their value intuitively because millions of years of evolution have trained our brains to know what feels right. So cultivate those instincts. They'll lead you to the writer's version of the Golden Rule: Reward readers as you would yourself.

Originally published in July–August 2021. Reprint R2104L

How High Achievers Overcome Their Anxiety

Strategies for escaping the most common "thought traps." *by Morra Aarons-Mele*

HERE'S A LITTLE SECRET: Some very successful people are wracked by anxiety. They worry about worst-case scenarios and every little thing that could go wrong. They stew over mistakes and unfavorably compare themselves with others. They focus on negative feedback while dismissing praise.

In many ways their anxiety is a benefit: After all, it fuels their drive, hard work, and achievement. They're prized employees precisely because they go the extra mile and are satisfied with nothing less than the best.

But if left unchecked, what may seem beneficial can make someone miserable, diminishing performance and career progress.

Consider Mark Goldstein, a lawyer. A few years ago he couldn't stop imagining catastrophes, such as being sued for malpractice. He also constantly measured himself against his peers. "Our firm has about 1,800 attorneys," he recalls, "and I thought the other 1,799 were all better able to deal with the stress of our jobs and lives." To compensate, he obsessively reviewed his emails for mistakes and worked through vacations.

Nihar Chhaya tells a similar story. Despite being named one of the top 100 executive coaches in the world by the leadership coach

Marshall Goldsmith, Chhaya used to routinely imagine his business faltering and question whether he'd be better off at a bigger company rather than on his own. "In my mind everyone else had it perfect," he says. "I was the one who wasn't going to excel."

I'll confess that I suffer from the same affliction. Recently asked to join an invitation-only business-book authors' group, I felt instant panic. Who was I to be included among these best-selling writers, popular TED speakers, and even a three-star general? My impostor syndrome was acute.

Many of us do this: succumb to what psychologists call *thought traps,* or what others call *cognitive distortion* or *thinking errors*—patterns of untrue and negatively biased thought so ingrained that they arise automatically to ensnare us. Then we can't see clearly, communicate effectively, or make good, reality-based decisions. And the consequences can have an adverse effect on us and the teams we lead.

Unfortunately, thought traps are exceedingly common among anxious achievers. To escape them, some people turn to overwork; others cope through drugs or alcohol, avoidance, or passive-aggressive behavior. But better solutions exist. The first step is to understand the various traps and identify which ones you're most prone to. Then you can take intentional, straightforward, research-backed steps to set yourself free.

Thought Traps and Escape Hatches

Eleven thought traps most commonly affect us at work—and you can escape each in specific ways. Most of these examples come from David Burns's classic *Feeling Good: The New Mood Therapy* and *The Feeling Good Handbook*, though I've included a few others that seem to particularly affect anxious achievers.

All-or-nothing thinking.
Burns describes this as a tendency to view things as black or white. If a situation falls short of perfection in your eyes, for example, you might see it as a total failure. A common example is a job interview. All-or-nothing thinkers will leave the interview focusing on a single

Idea in Brief

The Problem

A surprising number of extremely successful people are often wracked by anxiety. They suffer from common thought traps: negatively biased and untrue patterns of thought that arrive automatically and often prevent them from seeing clearly, communicating effectively, or making good, reality-based decisions. To deal with thought traps, some anxious achievers turn to overwork, others to coping mechanisms such as substance use, avoidance, or passive-aggressiveness.

The Solution

There are effective strategies for overcoming these thought traps. If we harness our anxiety and lessen its personal toll, we will help ourselves work with more energy and ingenuity. We will perform and feel better, become leaders whom people want to work for, and take the visionary risks needed to create positive change. We will achieve the same if not greater career success—without feeling constantly stressed out.

blunder they committed or the one thing they wish they'd said and conclude that the entire event was a bust. It's healthier to consider the interview as a whole: Sure, you wish you'd done a few things differently, but by and large it went OK. One of the best ways to respond to all-or-nothing thinking is to replace the "or" with "and." The interview had positive *and* negative moments. It was a mixture of good *and* bad.

When you're convinced that something is a complete disaster and nothing else, reach out to a trusted adviser. I usually turn to my husband or my former business partner. Both know me well and have a knack for helping me see in shades of gray rather than in my natural perfection-or-failure mindset.

Labeling.

According to Burns, labeling is an extreme form of all-or-nothing thinking: "Instead of saying, 'I made a mistake,' you attach a negative label to yourself: 'I'm a loser.'" We all have our own go-to labels when it comes to criticizing ourselves: "failure," "incompetent," "unqualified," "undeserving."

When you ascribe the source of a problem to someone's character rather than to that person's thinking or behavior, it suggests that the

61

situation cannot be improved. If you think you're inherently bad (*I am a failure*) rather than a normal person who makes mistakes or bad decisions (*I occasionally fail*), you've essentially given up. The same occurs when you label others. "You see them as totally bad," Burns writes. "This makes you feel hostile and . . . leaves little room for constructive communication."

One of the best ways to combat this thought trap (and others) is to use balanced thinking to examine the case for and against your knee-jerk assumption. Suppose you make a poor decision, and your automatic thought is *I'm such an idiot!* First, what's the evidence that you're an idiot? In this instance it's that you made the wrong call. Describe the mistake. Now consider: Is a single bad choice really proof that you're an idiot? Of course not. Documenting the opposing view also helps. Is there any evidence to indicate that you're *not* an idiot? I think you'll find plenty of things that attest to your competence and skill. If this balanced thinking points to areas in which you could improve—and they're the ones making you anxious—it's simply a sign to pay attention and put in more effort.

Jumping to conclusions.
This familiar thought trap takes two forms. One is mind reading, which occurs when you arbitrarily conclude that someone is reacting negatively to you. (*He doesn't think I deserve my promotion. I'm sure she hates me.*) The other is fortune-telling, which involves predicting that things will turn out badly even in the absence of proof. That can lead to inaction. (*Why bother trying?*)

I once thought a colleague was angry with me because she didn't smile when we passed in the hallway. It turned out that she was worried and unhappy because her kids were sick. I've also walked into presentations assuming that I was going to flub them—which made me more likely to do so. Indeed, both modes of jumping to conclusions can diminish self-esteem, productivity, relationships, and decision-making.

You can counteract this thought trap with truth. Ask yourself: "Do I have access to another person's inner thoughts? Can I really know what's going to happen in the future?" You can also remind yourself of times in the past when you jumped to conclusions and were proved wrong.

Catastrophizing.
This thought trap involves reaching the worst possible conclusion on the basis of little or no evidence: That tiny blemish must be melanoma. An argument with your significant other signals the end of the relationship. A less-than-perfect performance review means you'll be fired. A catastrophist always expects the worst-case scenario, no matter the issue.

Again, this sort of thinking undermines performance. Suppose a cash-flow analysis of your business is less positive than you expected. All of a sudden you're worried that the company will tank and you'll lose your job. Although your rational brain knows that's highly unlikely, when you're stuck in this thought trap, even the most outlandish scenario seems plausible. At this point, consider advice from the award-winning author Ashley C. Ford: Anxiety is an unreliable narrator that "lies to you and tells you that everything is going to go wrong all the time." She recommends reminding yourself that "feelings are not facts."

If you're finding it hard to reason your way out of irrationality, try taking a small but meaningful action to stop the mental spiral. Consult an impartial observer who can talk you down. Or try to move the needle just a tiny bit forward—away from catastrophe. Even a small amount of progress can nudge your brain to refocus and get back to productive work. Keep your attention on what you can do in the near term rather than on what might happen next year or even three months from now.

Filtering.
Burns describes mental filtering this way: "You pick out a single negative detail and dwell on it exclusively, so that your vision of all reality becomes darkened, like the drop of ink that discolors a beaker of water." As an example, he cites a presenter who gets lots of positive feedback about her talk but ignores it and instead obsesses over one colleague's critical comment.

Of course, the reverse can happen too—people may focus on what's gone right and turn a blind eye to what hasn't—but anxious achievers are more likely to dwell on the negative and fail to recognize and capitalize on all the things we do well. That leads to feeling discouraged or even hopeless.

A practical way to break out of this trap is to keep a record of your accomplishments and the praise you receive. Make a note every time you hit or exceed a target or log a win for your team or company, and retain any emails, tweets, or messages that contain positive feedback. That will provide objective proof that you're doing good work, and you can review your file whenever you're feeling overwhelmed or doubtful. (Bonus benefit: An achievement log makes self-assessments and performance reviews a snap.)

Discounting the positive.
This thought trap is very similar to filtering, but I call it out because it shows up so frequently in anxious achievers. I've heard many leaders dismiss their successes by insisting that they were a fluke resulting from luck or good timing or that anyone could have accomplished what they did.

That may appear to be humility and thus not as harmful as some of the other traps, but it can cause big problems if it prevents you from repeating a triumph or trying something new. For example, a former colleague of mine fears public speaking; even though she has delivered well-received presentations, she believes that each one is a fluke, so she passes up desirable opportunities that require a more public role.

"Should" statements.
I should be further along in my career by now. It shouldn't be so hard to get ahead at this company. I should know better. Examples of this very common thought trap, which occurs when reality hasn't met your high hopes or expectations, are endless. Statements that include the word "should" or its close relatives "must," "ought to," and "have to" can damage your mood and motivation, because, as Burns writes, they leave you feeling frustrated and rebellious rather than equipped to make changes and move toward your goals.

When you find yourself making a "should" statement, try reframing it in a gentler, less demanding way. For example, instead of *I should be further along in my career by now,* try *I'd like to be further along in my career.* Then consider whether there are actions you could take to rectify the problem. If there are, pursue them. If there aren't, you might realize that your "should" statement is unrealistic. For example, *I should always be able to anticipate my boss's needs* is an impossible standard.

Social comparison.

Comparing yourself with others is particularly pernicious, especially when it results in fatalistic self-assessments: *He'll always have higher sales than I do. She'll always earn more money.* At work the result is unhealthy competition and heightened anxiety, which stymie collaboration and collective performance.

To reset, turn comparison into curiosity. For example, Chhaya says he's trained himself to think, *Oh, wow, that's an interesting thing they're doing. Why not try that?* or *Hey, that's worked for them but it's not really what I want to do.* The key is to focus on who you are and what you want to accomplish rather than get anxious and distracted by others' achievements.

Personalization and blaming.

These are opposite expressions of the same error in thinking. Personalization occurs when you hold yourself responsible for circumstances and actions that are out of your control. For example, if one of your direct reports is struggling, you take it as evidence that you're a bad manager. Psychologists believe that we may fall into this thought trap to give ourselves the illusion of control, to avoid conflict, or to replicate a submissiveness learned in childhood.

Blaming, by contrast, consists of attributing the problem entirely to others: It's your employee's fault that he can't handle the workload. You can't understand why he doesn't observe the same high standards that you do.

A healthier response is to recognize that the truth probably lies somewhere in between—or at least requires more investigation. In a case like the one just mentioned, for instance, you should meet with your direct report, ask him what he thinks might be causing the problem, and then strategize together about potential solutions.

Ruminating.

This involves obsessive, repetitive thoughts about negative events in the past, problems we're having in the present, or ones we anticipate in the future. It is a huge anxiety amplifier, and it's all too common. Who hasn't mentally replayed a careless comment, a bad decision, a hurtful incident, or a failed comeback over and over again? Who hasn't become so fixated on a challenge at work or in a relationship that it drowns out everything else?

What distinguishes rumination from helpful processing is that it doesn't provide new ways of thinking, behaving, or solving the problem. It just covers the same territory again and again, keeping us locked in a negative mindset. Future-focused rumination may *feel* good: If you're worried about a tough task, you'll work harder at it; if you're fretting about a bad outcome, you'll try your best to avoid it. But it doesn't really work that way. Obsessing will almost always leave you languishing in a pattern of inaction.

One way I interrupt ruminating is by writing my thoughts down so that I can better see when they're irrational or illogical. That motivates me to move on.

Emotional reasoning.

This trap can be summed up as *I feel it, therefore it must be true.* For example: *I feel terrified about going on airplanes; it must be very dangerous to fly.* But any psychologist will tell you that feelings are actually a product of thoughts and beliefs, and if our thoughts are biased, the emotions we experience because of them won't reflect reality.

At work, emotional reasoning might show up as something like *I feel really overwhelmed by my workload, so I'm not capable of handling my job.* Unfortunately, it can drive you to an unhealthy response and become self-fulfilling. For example, if you react to feeling overwhelmed with avoidance or procrastination, you've made a bad situation worse.

Instead, as with other thought traps, you need to do what you can to get out of your head. Talk to an impartial observer and run a truth test on instances of emotional reasoning. Your feelings of incompetence, for example, are very likely to be exaggerated or false.

Dodging the Traps

I've already offered some advice on how to deal with each specific thought trap, but several overarching practices can help you avoid or escape all of them. (For most anxious achievers, I also recommend working with a good therapist.)

Make the anxiety an ally.

When harnessed, this complicated emotion can become a useful source of information and ultimately a leadership advantage—but only if you better understand it. Ask yourself probing questions such as "What exactly is worrying me?" "Is it a person, a situation, or a potential outcome?" "Why am I anxious about that?"

When you identify the true source of your anxiety, you can stop acting reflexively and work with intention and focus. Chhaya says he has made peace with his "neurotic" self: "I came to grips with the fact that . . . this is my natural tendency and in some ways it does me a service, because it makes me think in advance about a lot of issues."

Practice self-compassion.

As the psychology professor Kristin Neff has shown, replacing "self-judgment" with "self-kindness" can greatly reduce anxiety. If you approach yourself more positively, you'll feel better, think more clearly, and escape the thought traps.

Here's one exercise: Think of something you did well recently. Maybe you reached a successful outcome at work, had a thoughtful exchange with a friend, or even squeezed a workout into a busy day. Now tell yourself, *I did a good job*—and try to really feel it. Don't jump to a negative thought or a criticism or the next item on your to-do list. Bask in your accomplishment for just a bit.

See the humor.
Some thought traps are truly funny if we follow them to their logical conclusions: Will your typo actually cause you to get fired? Could it possibly be solely your fault that your company didn't meet its sales goals? Of course not! If you can acknowledge that absurdity and let it amuse you, you can immediately loosen the thought trap's grip. Defang your anxiety by learning to laugh about it.

Get physical.
Sometimes the best way to get out of your own head is to move your body. Run up some stairs. Stand up and stretch. Put on some music and dance. Even writing things down instead of just thinking about them can create some brain-body separation.

Try guided meditation.
Experts have long recommended meditation as a way to reduce anxiety, but I've found that when I'm really stuck in a thought trap, a silent meditation practice quickly turns into ruminating—or catastrophizing, or filtering, or labeling, or whatever happens to be afflicting me that day. What may work better is guided meditation, in which another person talks you through it, thereby giving you something other than your unhelpful thinking to focus on. Magic happens when we can pause and reset.

Just say no.
This one may seem too simple, but it works. When you're in a thought trap, literally interrupt it by saying "No" or "Stop" or "No, thanks" or "Not today!" The more you engage in this habit, the stronger it becomes. Your brain will learn this cue to break free of an anxiety-fueled thought before it traps you.

Your Potential, Realized

To reach your full potential, you can't let thought traps keep you in their grip. Goldstein, for one, broke free after taking a leave of absence from work to learn mindfulness and self-compassion practices. His ambition and sometimes his anxiety are still there, but he is no longer catastrophizing and stuck as a result.

Chhaya has likewise figured out how to let evidence assuage his doubts and worries: "I've succeeded with the business over the past seven years and I'm busier than ever," he explains, so "now I'm able to say I'm going to be OK."

As for me, I'm the poster child for putting my anxious-achiever persona to good use. I host a podcast and have written a book about it, and I coach others just like me. My message is simple: If we harness our anxiety and lessen its personal toll, we will help ourselves work with more energy and ingenuity. We will perform and feel better, become leaders whom people want to work for, and take the visionary risks needed to create positive change. We will achieve the same if not greater career success—without feeling constantly stressed out.

Notes

Morra Aarons-Mele is the author of The Anxious Achiever: Turn Your Biggest Fears Into Your Leadership Superpower *(Harvard Business Review Press, 2023), from which this article is adapted.*

Originally published in March–April 2023. Reprint R2302L

How to Play to Your Strengths

by Laura Morgan Roberts, Gretchen Spreitzer,
Jane Dutton, Robert Quinn, Emily Heaphy, and
Brianna Barker Caza

MOST FEEDBACK ACCENTUATES the negative. During formal employee evaluations, discussions invariably focus on "opportunities for improvement," even if the overall evaluation is laudatory. Informally, the sting of criticism lasts longer than the balm of praise. Multiple studies have shown that people pay keen attention to negative information. For example, when asked to recall important emotional events, people remember four negative memories for every positive one. No wonder most executives give and receive performance reviews with all the enthusiasm of a child on the way to the dentist.

Traditional, corrective feedback has its place, of course; every organization must filter out failing employees and ensure that everyone performs at an expected level of competence. Unfortunately, feedback that ferrets out flaws can lead otherwise talented managers to overinvest in shoring up or papering over their perceived weaknesses, or forcing themselves onto an ill-fitting template. Ironically, such a focus on problem areas prevents companies from reaping the best performance from its people. After all, it's a rare baseball player who is equally good at every position. Why should a natural third baseman labor to develop his skills as a right fielder?

The alternative, as the Gallup Organization researchers Marcus Buckingham, Donald Clifton, and others have suggested, is to foster excellence in the third baseman by identifying and harnessing his unique strengths. It is a paradox of human psychology that while people remember criticism, they respond to praise. The former makes them defensive and therefore unlikely to change, while the latter produces confidence and the desire to perform better. Managers who build up their strengths can reach their highest potential. This positive approach does not pretend to ignore or deny the problems that traditional feedback mechanisms identify. Rather, it offers a separate and unique feedback experience that counterbalances negative input. It allows managers to tap into strengths they may or may not be aware of and so contribute more to their organizations.

During the past few years, we have developed a powerful tool to help people understand and leverage their individual talents. Called the Reflected Best Self (RBS) exercise, our method allows managers to develop a sense of their "personal best" in order to increase their future potential. The RBS exercise is but one example of new approaches springing from an area of research called positive organizational scholarship (POS). Just as psychologists know that people respond better to praise than to criticism, organizational behavior scholars are finding that when companies focus on positive attributes such as resilience and trust, they can reap impressive bottom-line returns. (For more on this research, visit the website of the University of Michigan's Center for Positive Organizations at www.bus.mich.edu/positive/.) Thousands of executives, as well as tomorrow's leaders enrolled in business schools around the world, have completed the RBS exercise.

In this article, we will walk you through the RBS exercise step-by-step and describe the insights and results it can yield. Before we proceed, however, a few caveats are in order. First, understand that the tool is not designed to stroke your ego; its purpose is to assist you in developing a plan for more effective action. (Without such a plan, you'll keep running in place.) Second, the lessons generated from the RBS exercise can elude you if you don't pay sincere attention to them. If you are too burdened by time pressures and job

Idea in Brief

Most feedback accentuates the negative. During formal employee evaluations, discussions invariably focus on "opportunities for improvement," even if the overall evaluation is laudatory. No wonder most executives—and their direct reports—dread them.

Traditional, corrective feedback has its place, of course; every organization must filter out failing employees and ensure that everyone performs at an expected level of competence. But too much emphasis on problem areas prevents companies from reaping the best from their people. After all, it's a rare baseball player who is equally good at every position. Why should a natural third baseman labor to develop his skills as a right fielder?

This article presents a tool to help you understand and leverage your strengths. Called the Reflected Best Self (RBS) exercise, it offers a unique feedback experience that counterbalances negative input. It allows you to tap into talents you may or may not be aware of and so increase your career potential.

To begin the RBS exercise, you first need to solicit comments from family, friends, colleagues, and teachers, asking them to give specific examples of times in which your strengths were particularly beneficial. Next, you need to search for common themes in the feedback, organizing them in a table to develop a clear picture of your strong suits. Third, you must write a self-portrait—a description of yourself that summarizes and distills the accumulated information. And finally, you need to redesign your personal job description to build on what you're good at.

The RBS exercise will help you discover who you are at the top of your game. Once you're aware of your best self, you can shape the positions you choose to play—both now and in the next phase of your career.

demands, you may just file the information away and forget about it. To be effective, the exercise requires commitment, diligence, and follow-through. It may even be helpful to have a coach keep you on task. Third, it's important to conduct the RBS exercise at a different time of year than the traditional performance review so that negative feedback from traditional mechanisms doesn't interfere with the results of the exercise.

Used correctly, the RBS exercise can help you tap into unrecognized and unexplored areas of potential. Armed with a constructive, systematic process for gathering and analyzing data about your best self, you can burnish your performance at work.

Step 1: Identify Respondents and Ask for Feedback

The first task in the exercise is to collect feedback from a variety of people inside and outside work. By gathering input from a variety of sources—family members, past and present colleagues, friends, teachers, and so on—you can develop a much broader and richer understanding of yourself than you can from a standard performance evaluation.

As we describe the process of the Reflected Best Self exercise, we will highlight the experience of Robert Duggan (not his real name), whose self-discovery process is typical of the managers we've observed. Having retired from a successful career in the military at a fairly young age and earned an MBA from a top business school, Robert accepted a midlevel management position at an IT services firm. Despite strong credentials and leadership experience, Robert remained stuck in the same position year after year. His performance evaluations were generally good but not strong enough to put him on the high-potential track. Disengaged, frustrated, and disheartened, Robert grew increasingly stressed and disillusioned with his company. His workday felt more and more like an episode of *Survivor*.

Seeking to improve his performance, Robert enrolled in an executive education program and took the RBS exercise. As part of the exercise, Robert gathered feedback from 11 individuals from his past and present who knew him well. He selected a diverse but balanced group—his wife and two other family members, two friends from his MBA program, two colleagues from his time in the army, and four current colleagues.

Robert then asked these individuals to provide information about his strengths, accompanied by specific examples of moments when Robert used those strengths in ways that were meaningful to them, to their families or teams, or to their organizations. Many people—Robert among them—feel uncomfortable asking for exclusively

Requesting Feedback

HERE'S SOME SAMPLE LANGUAGE to use as you solicit feedback from family, friends, teachers, and colleagues.

Dear Colleague,

I'm currently working on creating a personal development plan. As part of that process, I'm gathering feedback from a variety of people I work with closely to help me develop a broader understanding of the strengths I bring to our work. I'm hoping you'll be willing to share your thoughts with me.

From your perspective, what would you say my professional strengths are? Just two or three would be helpful, and if you could cite specific examples of situations where I used those in ways that were meaningful to you, that would be great. Your candid feedback and examples will help me shape my development plan.

Thank you for taking the time to help me.

Sincerely,
X

positive feedback, particularly from colleagues. Accustomed to hearing about their strengths and weaknesses simultaneously, many executives imagine any positive feedback will be unrealistic, even false. Some also worry that respondents might construe the request as presumptuous or egotistical. But once managers accept that the exercise will help them improve their performance, they tend to dive in.

Within ten days, Robert received email responses from all 11 people describing specific instances when he had made important contributions—including pushing for high quality under a tight deadline, being inclusive in communicating with a diverse group, and digging for critical information. The answers he received surprised him. As a military veteran and a technical person holding an MBA, Robert rarely yielded to his emotions. But in reading story after story from his respondents, Robert found himself deeply moved—as if he were listening to appreciative speeches at a party thrown in his honor. The stories were also surprisingly convincing. He had more strengths than he knew. (For more on Step 1, refer to the sidebar "Gathering Feedback.")

Gathering Feedback

A CRITICAL STEP in the Reflected Best Self exercise involves soliciting feedback from family, friends, teachers, and colleagues. Email is an effective way of doing this, not only because it's comfortable and fast but also because it's easy to cut and paste responses into an analysis table such as the one in the sidebar "Finding common themes."

Below is the feedback Robert, a manager we observed, received from a current colleague and from a former coworker in the army.

From: Amy Chen

To: Robert Duggan

Subject: Re: Request for feedback

Dear Robert,

One of the greatest ways that you add value is that you stand for doing the right thing. For example, I think of the time that we were behind on a project for a major client and quality began to slip. You called a meeting and suggested that we had a choice: We could either pull a C by satisfying the basic requirements, or we could pull an A by doing excellent work. You reminded us that we could contribute to a better outcome. In the end, we met our deadline, and the client was very happy with the result.

From: Mike Bruno

To: Robert Duggan

Subject: Re: Request for feedback

One of the greatest ways you add value is that you persist in the face of adversity. I remember the time that we were both leading troops under tight security. We were getting conflicting information from the ground and from headquarters. You pushed to get the ground and HQ folks to talk to each other despite the tight time pressure. That information saved all of our lives. You never lost your calm, and you never stopped expecting or demanding the best from everyone involved.

Step 2: Recognize Patterns

In this step, Robert searched for common themes among the feedback, adding to the examples with observations of his own, then organizing all the input into a table. (To view parts of Robert's table, see the exhibit "Finding common themes.") Like many who participate in the RBS exercise, Robert expected that, given the diversity of respondents, the comments he received would be inconsistent or even competing. Instead, he was struck by their uniformity. The comments from his wife and family members were similar to those

Finding common themes

Creating a table helps you make sense of the feedback you collect. By clustering examples, you can more easily compare responses and identify common themes.

Common theme	Examples given	Possible interpretation
Ethics, values, and courage	• I take a stand when superiors and peers cross the boundaries of ethical behavior. • I am not afraid to stand up for what I believe in. I confront people who litter or who yell at their kids in public.	• I am at my best when I choose the harder right over the easier wrong. I derive even more satisfaction when I am able to teach others. I am professionally courageous.
Curiosity and perseverance	• I gave up a promising career in the military to get my MBA. • I investigated and solved a security breach through an innovative approach.	• I like meeting new challenges. I take risks and persevere despite obstacles.
Ability to build teams	• In high school, I assembled a team of students that helped improve the school's academic standards. • I am flexible and willing to learn from others, and I give credit where credit is due.	• I thrive when working closely with others.

from his army buddies and work colleagues. Everyone took note of Robert's courage under pressure, high ethical standards, perseverance, curiosity, adaptability, respect for diversity, and team-building skills. Robert suddenly realized that even his small, unconscious behaviors had made a huge impression on others. In many cases, he had forgotten about the specific examples cited until he read the feedback, because his behavior in those situations had felt like second nature to him.

The RBS exercise confirmed Robert's sense of himself, but for those who are unaware of their strengths, the exercise can be truly illuminating. Edward, for example, was a recently minted MBA executive in an automotive firm. His colleagues and subordinates were older and more experienced than he, and he felt uncomfortable disagreeing with them. But he learned through the RBS exercise that his peers appreciated his candid alternative views and respected the diplomatic and respectful manner with which he made his assertions. As a result, Edward grew bolder in making the case for his ideas, knowing that his boss and colleagues listened to him, learned from him, and appreciated what he had to say.

Other times, the RBS exercise sheds a more nuanced light on the skills one takes for granted. Beth, for example, was a lawyer who negotiated on behalf of nonprofit organizations. Throughout her life, Beth had been told she was a good listener, but her exercise respondents noted that the interactive, empathetic, and insightful manner in which she listened made her particularly effective. The specificity of the feedback encouraged Beth to take the lead in future negotiations that required delicate and diplomatic communications.

For naturally analytical people, the analysis portion of the exercise serves both to integrate the feedback and develop a larger picture of their capabilities. Janet, an engineer, thought she could study her feedback as she would a technical drawing of a suspension bridge. She saw her "reflected best self" as something to interrogate and improve. But as she read the remarks from family, friends, and colleagues, she saw herself in a broader and more human context. Over time, the stories she read about her enthusiasm and love of design helped her rethink her career path toward more managerial roles in which she might lead and motivate others.

Step 3: Compose Your Self-Portrait

The next step is to write a description of yourself that summarizes and distills the accumulated information. The description should weave themes from the feedback together with your self-observations into a composite of who you are at your best. The self-portrait is not designed to be a complete psychological and cognitive profile. Rather, it should be an insightful image that you can use as a reminder of your previous contributions and as a guide for future action. The portrait itself should not be a set of bullet points but rather a prose composition beginning with the phrase, "When I am at my best, I . . ." The process of writing out a two- to four-paragraph narrative cements the image of your best self in your consciousness. The narrative form also helps you draw connections between the themes in your life that may previously have seemed disjointed or unrelated. Composing the portrait takes time and demands careful consideration, but at the end of this process, you should come away with a rejuvenated image of who you are.

In developing his self-portrait, Robert drew on the actual words that others used to describe him, rounding out the picture with his own sense of himself at his best. He excised competencies that felt off the mark. This didn't mean he discounted them, but he wanted to assure that the overall portrait felt authentic and powerful. "When I am at my best," Robert wrote,

> I stand by my values and can get others to understand why doing so is important. I choose the harder right over the easier wrong. I enjoy setting an example. When I am in learning mode and am curious and passionate about a project, I can work intensely and untiringly. I enjoy taking things on that others might be afraid of or see as too difficult. I'm able to set limits and find alternatives when a current approach is not working. I don't always assume that I am right or know best, which engenders respect from others. I try to empower and give credit to others. I am tolerant and open to differences.

As Robert developed his portrait, he began to understand why he hadn't performed his best at work: He lacked a sense of mission. In the army, he drew satisfaction from the knowledge that the safety of the men and women he led, as well as the nation he served, depended on the quality of his work. He enjoyed the sense of teamwork and variety of problems to be solved. But as an IT manager in charge of routine maintenance on new hardware products, he felt bored and isolated from other people.

The portrait-writing process also helped Robert create a more vivid and elaborate sense of what psychologists would call his "possible self"—not just the person he is in his day-to-day job but the person he might be in completely different contexts. Organizational researchers have shown that when we develop a sense of our best possible self, we are better able to make positive changes in our lives.

Step 4: Redesign Your Job

Having pinpointed his strengths, Robert's next step was to redesign his personal job description to build on what he was good at. Given the fact that routine maintenance work left him cold, Robert's challenge was to create a better fit between his work and his best self. Like most RBS participants, Robert found that the strengths the exercise identified could be put into play in his current position. This involved making small changes in the way he worked, in the composition of his team, and in the way he spent his time. (Most jobs have degrees of freedom in all three of these areas; the trick is operating within the fixed constraints of your job to redesign work at the margins, allowing you to better play to your strengths.)

Robert began by scheduling meetings with systems designers and engineers who told him they were having trouble getting timely information flowing between their groups and Robert's maintenance team. If communication improved, Robert believed, new products would not continue to be saddled with the serious and costly maintenance issues seen in the past. Armed with a carefully documented history of those maintenance problems as well as a new understanding of his naturally analytical and creative team-building skills, Robert began meeting regularly with the designers and engineers to brainstorm better ways to prevent problems with new products. The meetings satisfied two of Robert's deepest best-self needs: He was interacting with more people at work, and he was actively learning about systems design and engineering.

Robert's efforts did not go unnoticed. Key executives remarked on his initiative and his ability to collaborate across functions, as well as on the critical role he played in making new products more reliable. They also saw how he gave credit to others. In less than nine months, Robert's hard work paid off, and he was promoted to program manager. In addition to receiving more pay and higher visibility, Robert enjoyed his work more. His passion was reignited; he felt intensely alive and authentic. Whenever he felt down or lacking in energy, he reread the original email feedback he had received. In difficult situations, the email messages helped him feel more resilient.

Robert was able to leverage his strengths to perform better, but there are cases in which RBS findings conflict with the realities of a person's job. This was true for James, a sales executive who told us he was "in a world of hurt" over his work situation. Unable to meet his ambitious sales goals, tired of flying around the globe to fight fires, his family life on the verge of collapse, James had suffered enough. The RBS exercise revealed that James was at his best when managing people and leading change, but these natural skills did not and could not come into play in his current job. Not long after he did the exercise, he quit his high-stress position and started his own successful company.

Other times, the findings help managers aim for undreamed-of positions in their own organizations. Sarah, a high-level administrator at a university, shared her best-self portrait with key colleagues, asking them to help her identify ways to better exploit her strengths and talents. They suggested that she would be an ideal candidate for a new executive position. Previously, she would never have considered applying for the job, believing herself unqualified. To her surprise, she handily beat out the other candidates.

Beyond Good Enough

We have noted that while people remember criticism, awareness of faults doesn't necessarily translate into better performance. Based on that understanding, the RBS exercise helps you remember your strengths—and construct a plan to build on them. Knowing your strengths also offers you a better understanding of how to deal with your weaknesses—and helps you gain the confidence you need to address them. It allows you to say, "I'm great at leading but lousy at numbers. So rather than teach me remedial math, get me a good finance partner." It also allows you to be clearer in addressing your areas of weakness as a manager. When Tim, a financial services executive, received feedback that he was a great listener and coach, he also became more aware that he had a tendency to spend too much time being a cheerleader and too little time keeping his employees to task. Susan, a senior advertising executive, had the opposite problem: While her feedback lauded her results-oriented management approach, she wanted to be sure that she hadn't missed opportunities to give her employees the space to learn and make mistakes.

In the end, the strength-based orientation of the RBS exercise helps you get past the "good enough" bar. Once you discover who you are at the top of your game, you can use your strengths to better shape the positions you choose to play—both now and in the next phase of your career.

Originally published in January 2005. Reprint R0501G

You're Not Powerless in the Face of Imposter Syndrome

Research found that moxie—strength of will, self-discipline, and the ability to persist despite challenges—was vital to the success of professionals from underrepresented backgrounds.

by Keith D. Dorsey

"I WAS INTIMIDATED FOR MANY YEARS in the early part of my board career because I didn't have a business degree and felt under-prepared," a female board director once told me. Another director, explaining that she "grew up in the shadows of a plantation" reflected, "It's still very much a white male show, so the fact that I was the first African American female on the board was astounding to me."

As U.S. practice leader of CEO and board services at Boyden, an executive search firm, I interact with hundreds of aspiring and existing directors. Questions about their qualifications for board service remain a concern for many of the people I talk to, particularly those from underrepresented backgrounds.

My experience aligns with research that shows that high achievers from underrepresented backgrounds often find themselves confronting imposter syndrome, or doubting their skills and achievements or fearing being exposed as a fraud.[1] Women and people of color may be more likely to feel they don't fit in, they're not welcome, and they don't belong.[2]

Imposter syndrome can be crippling mentally and emotionally, drain your energy and attention, and cause you to fall short of the performance you are capable of, thus feeding the cycle of self-doubt. If you experience imposter syndrome, you may explain away your successes by thinking anyone could have done what you did, or thinking you just got lucky, or fearing that others are mistaken in believing that you're talented. As if that isn't bad enough, when you stumble or face challenges, your self-perceived incompetence looms larger than life—increasing your chance of failure and perpetuating the syndrome.

While awareness of this cycle is helpful, understanding imposter syndrome does little to end it. Instead, you need action. And to take action, you need moxie.

Moxie: A Working Definition

Moxie reflects an intensity of motivation and is related to (but distinct from) traits such as grit, self-control, and the ability to overcome procrastination.[3] The term was popularized by a 1920s soft drink advertised to give its drinkers vigor, nerve, and pep. After Boston Red Sox player Ted Williams endorsed the drink, moxie entered the cultural consciousness as shorthand for strength, aggressiveness, skill, and know-how.

In my own research, I've seen that the attributes of moxie—strength of will, self-discipline, and the ability to persist despite challenges—was vital to underrepresented directors' success.[4] One Latina executive I spoke with described moxie in this way: "I noticed my Black colleagues overcoming the objections coming at them in their careers. Whenever they set goals, they achieved them. They had a 'refuse to lose' mentality. And once I emulated what I saw in them, I rapidly ascended the corporate ladder myself."

The directors I interviewed explained that they neither internalized the obstacles they encountered as personal failures nor externalized them as irreconcilable systemic barriers. In fact, when

Idea in Brief

The Problem

Research shows that high achievers from underrepresented backgrounds often find themselves confronting imposter syndrome or feeling they don't fit in, are not welcome, or don't belong. But understanding imposter syndrome does little to end it.

The Solution

The attributes of moxie—strength of will, self-discipline, and the ability to persist despite challenges—are vital to the success of executives from underrepresented backgrounds. These people can take four tactics to help build their moxie: utilizing strengths forged through culture-based hardships; giving themselves permission to play; tuning out naysayers; and recognizing when to walk away.

I asked them to identify the barriers they faced, it took them a while to recall and identify them because they had transformed their obstacles into sources of motivation. It became apparent that moxie was a response to their childhood experiences of racism, sexism, microaggression, and other difficulties.

If you are a woman or person of color and you want to push forward and advance in your career, you will encounter obstacles and you will experience failure. At these times, you have a choice to make: Will you allow the obstacles and failures to feed imposter syndrome, or will you pick yourself up and use moxie to persist toward your goal?

If you choose moxie, you may not be disappointed. In a study by psychology professor Jessica Curtis and colleagues, moxie was found to predict intrinsic and extrinsic motivation more than other motivational constructs like grit or self-control.[5] Moxie also predicted goal achievement—largely because people with moxie invest more resources into their aims. For example, one director I interviewed realized that her career choice of spending years as a consultant and then becoming CEO of a small company created substantial obstacles to her landing a corporate board seat. "Boards still tend to recruit against a checklist of wanting a sitting CEO of a multinational corporation," she explained. "So when I'd approach recruiters, they would push back with, 'Ooo . . . ah . . . I'll *really* have to convince the board that it is worth it for them to speak with you.'" At this point, she could have agreed with others' opinions that she wasn't boardroom material. Instead, she recognized the need to translate her experiences and skills into language a board would understand and find attractive. Now, only a few years into board service, she sits on three publicly traded company boards and three nonprofit boards.

Making Moxie Your Superpower

Based on the experiences of the underrepresented directors I interviewed in my study and the aspiring and existing directors I continue to interact with, I suggest four tactics to help you make moxie your very own superpower:

1. Utilize the strengths you've forged through culture-based hardships.

People of color have endured centuries of hardship and oppression, and through these we have forged attitudes and approaches that give us unique advantages, as research regarding racism-related coping and posttraumatic growth following racial trauma has shown.[6] Tabitha Grier-Reed and colleagues at the University of Minnesota have found that deepening your connections with others, harnessing inner strengths, developing fresh perspectives and appreciation for life, and connecting with your spirituality, in particular, help you grow and flourish in your career and life.[7]

One Black women board member I interviewed explained that her grandparents had raised her to understand the inequity of opportunities presented to people of color. As a result, she persisted through barriers because, as she put it, "I had no choice. Like other women of my generation, we were told by our parents and grandparents to just get out there and do it. Make it happen. If you're given an opportunity, demonstrate to them that you deserve the opportunity." Similarly, the other directors I interviewed explained that they learned to ignore, go under, go over, go around, or go through any obstacles put in front of them—in other words, they used moxie.

To turn your own hardships into moxie, identify a challenging situation from your past that you ultimately overcame. Reflect on how you got through it and how you resolved the situation. Finally, articulate the principles you learned and strengths you gained. Together, these are some ingredients of your unique brand of moxie.

For example, women and students of color commonly report facing negative stereotypes when enrolling in STEM courses.[8] One such woman recalled, "I had to take organic chemistry, but without the years of preparatory courses all my classmates had. So I had lots of questions that seemed very elementary to others. As a result, everyone—students, lecturers, and my mentor—thought I didn't belong there and refused to help me." To overcome this formidable challenge, she explained, "I spent many sleepless nights reading extra material, going over class notes and homework multiple times, and slowly caught up. I ultimately graduated from my degree program with one of the highest grades." From this experience, this young woman recognized that she relished a challenge and realized she could rely on her strengths of a strong work ethic, self-discipline, focus, and an ability to learn unfamiliar scientific material with limited support. This moxie continued to help her flourish in her career.

2. Give yourself permission to play.

Herminia Ibarra, professor at London Business School, has conducted extensive research on what she calls "identity play," which involves experimenting with new ideas and behaviors as you take on new professional challenges and roles.[9] She uses the term "play" to normalize the idea that you won't perform as well in the new role as you do in more familiar roles.

Importantly, play is not a "fake it till you make it" situation. Instead, it's about authentically growing into new roles by trying new behaviors, gaining confidence, and allowing yourself time and space for development. This was a critical tactic for one director I interviewed, who explained, "Debt financing, bond markets, and the investor base were foreign concepts to me. So when these came up, I reminded myself that I had to have just enough knowledge to stay on the stage, and I kept trying and focused on being a learner."

To foster your own identity play, think of a work situation where you are still on a learning curve. Break the situation or role into a series of small learning experiences with deliberate action planning, experimentation, and data gathering on your performance. Then repeat the cycle.

3. Tune out the naysayers.

If you are working hard to achieve much in your career and life, you are bound to encounter naysayers who are more than eager to point out the ways you don't measure up. The late Kaleel Jamison, a pioneering career woman in 1970s corporate America, called these messages "nibbles" intended to make you smaller.

When you agree with the nibble (or, worse, initiate the nibble yourself), you feed the imposter syndrome. I recently witnessed this in a young and talented mentee of mine who has been spearheading transformative change in her company despite having taken her role only months ago. While her proposed initiative had been blessed by her boss and her CEO, another leader above her blocked her with, "Well, your plan is completely unworkable." She slid into a pit of paralyzing self-doubt. Having seen the plan myself, I knew the criticism was unfounded but suspected there was more to the story. Once we debriefed on the situation, I realized that she had circulated her plan in a way that inadvertently criticized the leader's work, resulting in a predictable backlash. We then discussed more effective ways to solicit support from the various stakeholders involved—including the leader in question. She then created and implemented a more successful approach, in turn learning from this experience and strengthening her competencies.

When you experience criticism, begin by reframing it as a hypothesis (e.g., "The plan will not work"). Next, identify ways to test the hypothesis, such as by getting feedback from trusted mentors or conducting a low-risk proof of concept. Third, gather data and test the hypothesis. Regardless of the results, you will gain concrete and actionable feedback that will help you progress.

4. Recognize when to walk away.

Imposter syndrome often is used to mask systemic bias and racism in the workplace, as Ruchika Tulshyan and Jodi-Ann Burey have aptly noted.[10] This means that moxie won't work in every situation.

One director I interviewed had a longstanding dream to become the CEO at her employer. "I eventually realized that even though I was performing well, I couldn't control how the leadership decided who actually got C-suite opportunities and who didn't. So, I made the hard decision that I still wanted to be a CEO, but it didn't have to be there. And I left."

When you encounter an obstacle, take time to assess the competencies, energy, and passion you would need to overcome it, and then soberly evaluate whether you want to invest your resources in this way. For example, if you discover that success requires knowledge or skills you don't have and cannot realistically develop in the needed time frame, or if you cannot get the mentoring or advocacy you need to succeed, it may be wiser to walk away. When you deliberately evaluate the obstacles facing you, you will either take on the challenges fully informed or reallocate your abilities in more suitable environments.

I will be the first to admit that the steps I describe above are not easy. Turning away from imposter syndrome and embracing your moxie requires you to reexamine your assumptions, values, and beliefs; risk new behaviors; and commit more to yourself and your growth than you may ever have before. In other words, embracing moxie sets you on a path of transformative learning, which is rooted in the truism that growth comes from discomfort. As the old man in George Bernard Shaw's *Back to Methusaleh* noted, "Life is not meant to be easy, my child, but take courage, for it can be delightful."

Originally published on June 2, 2023. Reprint H07N00

Notes

1. Joe Langford and Pauline Rose Clance, "The Imposter Phenomenon: Recent Research Findings Regarding Dynamics, Personality and Family Patterns and Their Implications for Treatment," *Psychotherapy: Theory, Research, Practice, Training* 30, no. 3 (1993): 495–501.

2. Cara MacInnis, "Impostor Syndrome as a Diversity, Equity & Inclusion Issue," UCalgary Psychology Equity, Diversity and Inclusion Blog, February 12, 2020, https://www.ucalgary.ca/news/impostor-syndrome-diversity-equity-inclusion-issue.

3. Jessica Curtis et al., "Moxie: Individual Variability in Motivation Intensity," *Current Psychology* (2022).

4. Keith D. Dorsey, "Corporate Board Diversity: A Path to Board Service from the Wisdom of Black Women Directors" (PhD diss., University of Southern California, 2022).

5. Curtis et al., "Moxie."

6. Veronica E. Johnson and Robert T. Carter, "Black Cultural Strengths and Psychosocial Well-Being: An Empirical Analysis with Black American Adults," *Journal of Black Psychology* 46, no. 1 (2020): 55–89.

7. Tabitha Grier-Reed et al., "Posttraumatic Growth and Flourishing in the Face of Racial Trauma," *Psychological Trauma: Theory, Research, Practice, and Policy* 15, no. 1 (2023): 37–44.

8. Maria Temming, "STEM's Racial, Ethnic and Gender Gaps Are Still Strikingly Large," *Science News*, April 14, 2021, https://www.sciencenews.org/article/science-technology-math-race-ethnicity-gender-diversity-gap.

9. Herminia Ibarra, "Provisional Selves: Experimenting with Image and Identity in Professional Adaptation," *Administrative Science Quarterly* 44, no. 4 (1999): 764–791.

10. Ruchika Tulshyan and Jodi-Ann Burey, "Stop Telling Women They Have Imposter Syndrome," hbr.org, February 11, 2021.

The Feedback Fallacy

by Marcus Buckingham and Ashley Goodall

THE DEBATE ABOUT FEEDBACK AT WORK isn't new. Since at least the middle of the last century, the question of how to get employees to improve has generated a good deal of opinion and research. But recently the discussion has taken on new intensity.

The ongoing experiment in "radical transparency" at Bridgewater Associates and the culture at Netflix, which the *Wall Street Journal* recently described as "encouraging harsh feedback" and subjecting workers to "intense and awkward" real-time 360s, are but two examples of the overriding belief that the way to increase performance in companies is through rigorous, frequent, candid, pervasive, and often critical feedback.

How should we give and receive feedback? we wonder. How much, and how often, and using which new app? And, given the hoopla over the approaches of Bridgewater and Netflix, how hard-edged and fearlessly candid should we be? Behind those questions, however, is another question that we're missing, and it's a crucial one. The search for ways to give and receive better feedback assumes that feedback is always useful. But the only reason we're pursuing it is to help people do better. And when we examine *that*—asking, *How can we help each person thrive and excel?*—we find that the answers take us in a different direction.

To be clear, instruction—telling people what steps to follow or what factual knowledge they're lacking—can be truly useful: That's why we have checklists in airplane cockpits and, more recently, in operating rooms. There is indeed a right way for a nurse to give an injection safely, and if you as a novice nurse miss one of the steps, or if you're unaware of critical facts about a patient's condition, then someone should tell you. But the occasions when the actions or knowledge necessary to minimally perform a job can be objectively defined in advance are rare and becoming rarer. What we mean by "feedback" is very different. Feedback is about telling people what we think of their performance and how they should do it better—whether they're giving an effective presentation, leading a team, or creating a strategy. And on that, the research is clear: Telling people what we think of their performance doesn't help them thrive and excel, and telling people how we think they should improve actually *hinders* learning.

Underpinning the current conviction that feedback is an unalloyed good are three theories that we in the business world commonly accept as truths. The first is that other people are more aware than you are of your weaknesses, and that the best way to help you, therefore, is for them to show you what you cannot see for yourself. We can call this our *theory of the source of truth.* You do not realize that your suit is shabby, that your presentation is boring, or that your voice is grating, so it is up to your colleagues to tell you as plainly as possible "where you stand." If they didn't, you would never know, and this would be bad.

The second belief is that the process of learning is like filling up an empty vessel: You lack certain abilities you need to acquire, so your colleagues should teach them to you. We can call this our *theory of learning.* If you're in sales, how can you possibly close deals if you don't learn the competency of "mirroring and matching" the prospect? If you're a teacher, how can you improve if you don't learn and practice the steps in the latest team-teaching technique or "flipped classroom" format? The thought is that you can't—and that you need feedback to develop the skills you're missing.

And the third belief is that great performance is universal, analyzable, and describable, and that once defined, it can be transferred from one person to another, regardless of who each individual is. Hence you can, with feedback about what excellence looks like,

Idea in Brief

The Challenge

Managers today are bombarded with calls to give feedback—constantly, directly, and critically. But it turns out that telling people what we think of their performance and how they can do better is not the best way to help them excel and, in fact, can hinder development.

The Reality

Research shows that, first, we aren't the reliable raters of other people's performance that we

think we are; second, criticism inhibits the brain's ability to learn; and, third, excellence is idiosyncratic, can't be defined in advance, and isn't the opposite of failure. Managers can't "correct" a person's way to excellence.

The Solution

Managers need to help their team members see what's working, stopping them with a "Yes! That!" and sharing their experience of what the person did well.

understand where you fall short of this ideal and then strive to remedy your shortcomings. We can call this our *theory of excellence.* If you're a manager, your boss might show you the company's supervisor-behaviors model, hold you up against it, and tell you what you need to do to more closely hew to it. If you aspire to lead, your firm might use a 360-degree feedback tool to measure you against its predefined leadership competencies and then suggest various courses or experiences that will enable you to acquire the competencies that your results indicate you lack.

What these three theories have in common is self-centeredness: They take our own expertise and what we are sure is our colleagues' inexpertise as givens; they assume that my way is necessarily your way. But as it turns out, in extrapolating from what creates our own performance to what might create performance in others, we overreach.

Research reveals that none of these theories is true. The more we depend on them, and the more technology we base on them, the *less* learning and productivity we will get from others. To understand why and to see the path to a more effective way of improving performance, let's look more closely at each theory in turn.

The Source of Truth

The first problem with feedback is that humans are unreliable raters of other humans. Over the past 40 years psychometricians have shown in study after study that people don't have the objectivity to hold in their heads a stable definition of an abstract quality, such as *business acumen* or *assertiveness*, and then accurately evaluate someone else on it. Our evaluations are deeply colored by our own understanding of what we're rating others on, our own sense of what good looks like for a particular competency, our harshness or leniency as raters, and our own inherent and unconscious biases. This phenomenon is called the *idiosyncratic rater effect*, and it's large (more than half of your rating of someone else reflects your characteristics, not hers) and resilient (no training can lessen it). In other words, the research shows that feedback is more distortion than truth.

This is why, despite all the training available on how to *receive* feedback, it's such hard work: Recipients have to struggle through this forest of distortion in search of something that they recognize as themselves.

And because your feedback to others is always more you than them, it leads to systematic error, which is magnified when ratings are considered in aggregate. There are only two sorts of measurement error in the world: *random* error, which you can reduce by averaging many readings; and *systematic* error, which you can't. Unfortunately, we all seem to have left math class remembering the former and not the latter. We've built all our performance and leadership feedback tools as though assessment errors are random, and they're not. They're systematic.

Consider color blindness. If we ask a color-blind person to rate the redness of a particular rose, we won't trust his feedback—we know that he is incapable of seeing, let alone "rating," red. His error isn't random; it's predictable and explainable, and it stems from a flaw in his measurement system; hence, it's systematic. If we then decide to ask seven more color-blind people to rate the redness of our rose, their errors will be equally systematic, and averaging their ratings won't get us any closer to determining the actual redness of the rose.

In fact, it's worse than this. Adding up all the inaccurate redness ratings—"gray," "pretty gray," "whitish gray," "muddy brown," and so on—and averaging them leads us *further away* both from learning anything reliable about the individuals' personal experiences of the rose and from the actual truth of how red our rose really is.

What the research has revealed is that we're all color-blind when it comes to abstract attributes, such as *strategic thinking*, *potential*, and *political savvy*. Our inability to rate others on them is predictable and explainable—it is systematic. We cannot remove the error by adding more data inputs and averaging them out, and doing that actually makes the error bigger.

Worse still, although science has long since proven that we are color-blind, in the business world we assume we're clear-eyed. Deep down we don't think we make very many errors at all. We think we're reliable raters of others. We think we're a source of truth. We aren't. We're a source of error.

When a feedback instrument surveys eight colleagues about your business acumen, your score of 3.79 is far greater a distortion than if it simply surveyed one person about you—the 3.79 number is *all* noise, no signal. Given that (a) we're starting to see more of this sort of data-based feedback, (b) this data on you will likely be kept by your company for a very long time, and (c) it will be used to pay, promote, train, and deploy or fire you, you should be worried about just how fundamentally flawed it really is.

The only realm in which humans are an unimpeachable source of truth is that of their own feelings and experiences. Doctors have long known this. When they check up on you post-op, they'll ask, "On a scale of one to 10, with 10 being high, how would you rate your pain?" And if you say, "Five," the doctor may then prescribe all manner of treatments, but what she's unlikely to do is challenge you on your "five." It doesn't make sense, no matter how many operations she has done, to tell you your "five" is wrong, and that, actually, this morning your pain is a "three." It doesn't make sense to try to parse what you mean by "five," and whether any cultural differences might indicate that your "five" is not, in fact, a real "five." It doesn't make sense to hold calibration sessions with other doctors to ensure that your "five" is the same as the other "fives" in the rooms down the hall. Instead, she can be confident that you are the best judge of your pain and that all she can know for sure is that you will be feeling better when you rate your pain lower. Your rating is yours, not hers.

Just as your doctor doesn't know the truth of your pain, we don't know the truth about our colleagues, at least not in any objective way. You may read that workers today—especially Millennials—want to know where they stand. You may occasionally have team members ask you to tell them where they stand, objectively. You may feel that it's your duty to try to answer these questions. But you can't—none of us can. All we can do—and it's not nothing—is share our own feelings and experiences, our own reactions. Thus we can tell someone whether his voice grates *on us*; whether he's persuasive *to us*; whether his presentation is boring *to us*. We may not be able to tell him where he stands, but we can tell him where he stands *with us*. Those are our truths, not his. This is a humbler claim, but at least it's accurate.

How We Learn

Another of our collective theories is that feedback contains useful information, and that this information is the magic ingredient that will accelerate someone's learning. Again, the research points in the opposite direction. Learning is less a function of adding something that isn't there than it is of recognizing, reinforcing, and refining what already is. There are two reasons for this.

The first is that, neurologically, we grow more in our areas of greater ability (our strengths are our development areas). The brain continues to develop throughout life, but each person's does so differently. Because of your genetic inheritance and the oddities of your early childhood environment, your brain's wiring is utterly unique. Some parts of it have tight thickets of synaptic connections, while others are far less dense, and these patterns are different from one person to the next. According to brain science, people grow far more neurons and synaptic connections where they already have the most neurons and synaptic connections. In other words, each brain grows most where it's already strongest. As Joseph LeDoux, a professor of neuroscience at New York University, memorably described it, "Added connections are therefore more like new buds on a branch rather than new branches." Through this lens, learning looks a lot like building, little by little, on the unique patterns already there within you. Which in turn means learning has to start by finding and understanding those patterns—your patterns, not someone else's.

Second, getting attention to our strengths from others catalyzes learning, whereas attention to our weaknesses smothers it. Neurological science also shows what happens to us when other people focus on what's working within us instead of remediating what isn't. In one experiment scientists split students into two groups. To one group they gave positive coaching, asking the students about their dreams and how they'd go about achieving them. The scientists probed the other group about homework and what the students thought they were doing wrong and needed to fix. While those conversations were happening, the scientists hooked each student up to a functional magnetic resonance imaging machine to see which parts of the brain were most activated in response to these different sorts of attention.

In the brains of the students asked about what they needed to correct, the sympathetic nervous system lit up. This is the "fight or flight" system, which mutes the other parts of the brain and allows us to focus only on the information most necessary to survive. Your brain responds to critical feedback as a threat and narrows its activity. The strong negative emotion produced by criticism "inhibits access to existing neural circuits and invokes cognitive, emotional, and perceptual impairment," psychology and business professor Richard Boyatzis said in summarizing the researchers' findings.

Focusing people on their shortcomings or gaps doesn't enable learning. It impairs it.

In the students who focused on their dreams and how they might achieve them, the sympathetic nervous system was not activated. What lit up instead was the parasympathetic nervous system, sometimes referred to as the "rest and digest" system. To quote Boyatzis again: "The parasympathetic nervous system . . . stimulates adult neurogenesis (i.e., growth of new neurons) . . ., a sense of well-being, better immune system functioning, and cognitive, emotional, and perceptual openness."

What findings such as these show us is, first, that learning happens when we see how we might do something better by adding some new nuance or expansion to our own understanding. Learning rests on our grasp of what we're doing well, not on what we're doing poorly, and certainly not on someone else's sense of what we're doing poorly. And second, that we learn most when someone else pays attention to what's working within us and asks us to cultivate it intelligently. We're often told that the key to learning is to get out of our comfort zones, but these findings contradict that particular chestnut: Take us very far out of our comfort zones, and our brains stop paying attention to anything other than surviving the experience. It's clear that we learn most in our comfort zones, because that's where our neural pathways are most concentrated. It's where we're most open to possibility, most creative, insightful, and productive. That's where feedback must meet us—in our moments of flow.

Excellence

We spend the bulk of our working lives pursuing excellence in the belief that while defining it is easy, the really hard part is codifying how we and everyone else on our team should get there. We've got it backward: Excellence in any endeavor is almost impossible to define, and yet getting there, for each of us, is relatively easy.

Excellence is idiosyncratic. Take funniness—the ability to make others laugh. If you watch early Steve Martin clips, you might land on the idea that excellence at it means strumming a banjo, waggling your knees, and wailing, "I'm a wild and crazy guy!" But watch Jerry Seinfeld, and you might conclude that it means talking about nothing in a slightly annoyed, exasperated tone. And if you watch Sarah Silverman, you might think to yourself, no, it's being caustic, blunt, and rude in an incongruously affectless way. At this point you may begin to perceive the truth that "funny" is inherent to the person.

Watch an NBA game, and you may think to yourself, "Yes, most of them are tall and athletic, but boy, not only does each player have a different role on the team, but even the players in the same role on the same team seem to do it differently." Examine something as specific and as limited as the free throws awarded after fouls, and you'll learn that not only do the top two free-throw shooters in history have utterly different styles, but one of them, Rick Barry—the best ever on the day he retired (look him up)—didn't even throw overhand.

Excellence seems to be inextricably and wonderfully intertwined with whoever demonstrates it. Each person's version of it is uniquely shaped and is an expression of that person's individuality. Which means that, for each of us, excellence is easy, in that it is a natural, fluid, and intelligent expression of our best extremes. It can be cultivated, but it's unforced.

Excellence is also not the opposite of failure. But in virtually all aspects of human endeavor, people assume that it is and that if they study what leads to pathological functioning and do the reverse—or replace what they found missing—they can create optimal functioning. That assumption is flawed. Study disease and you will learn a lot about disease and precious little about health. Eradicating depression will get you no closer to joy. Divorce is mute on the topic of happy marriage. Exit interviews with employees who leave tell you nothing about why others stay. If you study failure, you'll learn a lot about failure but nothing about how to achieve excellence. Excellence has its own pattern.

And it's even more problematic than that. Excellence and failure often have a lot in common. So if you study ineffective leaders and observe that they have big egos, and then argue that good leaders should not have big egos, you will lead people astray. Why? Because when you do personality assessments with highly effective leaders, you discover that they have very strong egos as well. Telling someone that you must lose your ego to be a good leader is flawed advice. Likewise, if you study poor salespeople, discover that they take rejection personally, and then tell a budding salesperson to avoid doing the same, your advice will be misguided. Why? Because rigorous studies of the best salespeople reveal that they take rejection deeply personally, too.

As it happens, you find that effective leaders put their egos in the service of others, not themselves, and that effective salespeople take rejection personally because they are personally invested in the sale—but the point is that you will never find these things out by studying *ineffective* performance.

Since excellence is idiosyncratic and cannot be learned by studying failure, we can never help another person succeed by holding her performance up against a prefabricated model of excellence, giving her feedback on where she misses the model, and telling her to plug the gaps. That approach will only ever get her to adequate performance. Point out the grammatical flaws in an essay, ask the writer to fix the flaws, and while you may get an essay with good grammar, you won't get a piece of writing that transports the reader. Show a new teacher when her students lost interest and tell her what to do to fix this, and while you may now have a teacher whose students don't fall asleep in class, you won't have one whose students necessarily learn any more.

How to Help People Excel

If we continue to spend our time identifying failure as we see it and giving people feedback about how to avoid it, we'll languish in the business of adequacy. To get into the excellence business we need some new techniques:

Look for outcomes.

Excellence is an outcome, so take note of when a prospect leans into a sales pitch, a project runs smoothly, or an angry customer suddenly calms down. Then turn to the team member who created the outcome and say, "That! Yes, that!" By doing this, you'll stop the flow of work for a moment and pull your colleague's attention back toward something she just did that really worked.

There's a story about how legendary Dallas Cowboys coach Tom Landry turned around his struggling team. While the other teams were reviewing missed tackles and dropped balls, Landry instead

The Right Way to Help Colleagues Excel

IF YOU WANT to get into the excellence business, here are some examples of language to try.

Instead of	Try
Can I give you some feedback?	Here's my reaction.
Good job!	Here are three things that really worked for me. What was going through your mind when you did them?
Here's what you should do.	Here's what I would do.
Here's where you need to improve.	Here's what worked best for me, and here's why.
That didn't really work.	When you did x, I felt y or I didn't get that.
You need to improve your communication skills.	Here's exactly where you started to lose me.
You need to be more responsive.	When I don't hear from you, I worry that we're not on the same page.
You lack strategic thinking.	I'm struggling to understand your plan.
You should do x [in response to a request for advice].	What do you feel you're struggling with, and what have you done in the past that's worked in a similar situation?

combed through footage of previous games and created for each player a highlight reel of when he had done something easily, naturally, and effectively. Landry reasoned that while the number of wrong ways to do something was infinite, the number of right ways, for any particular player, was not. It was knowable, and the best way to discover it was to look at plays where that person had done it excellently. From now on, he told each team member, "we only replay your winning plays."

Now on one level he was doing this to make his team members feel better about themselves because he knew the power of praise. But according to the story, Landry wasn't nearly as interested in praise as he was in learning. His instincts told him that each person would improve his performance most if he could see, in slow motion, what his own personal version of excellence looked like.

You can do the same. Whenever you see one of your people do something that worked for you, that rocked your world just a little, stop for a minute and highlight it. By helping your team member recognize what excellence looks like for her—by saying, "That! Yes, that!"—you're offering her the chance to gain an insight; you're highlighting a pattern that is already there within her so that she can recognize it, anchor it, re-create it, and refine it. That is learning.

Replay your instinctive reactions.
Unlike Landry, you're not going to be able to videotape your people. Instead, learn how to replay to them your own personal reactions. The key is not to tell someone how well she's performed or how good she is. While simple praise isn't a bad thing, you are by no means the authority on what objectively good performance is, and instinctively she knows this. Instead, describe what you experienced when her moment of excellence caught your attention. There's nothing more believable and more authoritative than sharing what you saw from her and how it made you feel. Use phrases such as "This is how that came across for me," or "This is what that made me think," or even just "Did you see what you did there?" Those are your reactions—they are your truth—and when you relay them in specific detail, you aren't judging or rating or fixing her; you're simply reflecting to her the unique "dent" she just made in the world, as seen through your eyes. And precisely because it isn't a judgment or a rating, it is at once more humble and more powerful.

On the flip side, if you're the team member, whenever your team leader catches you doing something right, ask her to pause and describe her reaction to you. If she says, "Good job!" ask, "Which bit? What did you see that seemed to work well?" Again, the point of this isn't to pile on the praise. The point is to explore the nature of excellence, and this is surely a better object for all the energy currently being pointed at "radical transparency" and the like. We're so close to our own performance that it's hard to get perspective on it and see its patterns and components. Ask for your leader's help in rendering the unconscious, conscious—so that you can understand it, improve at it, and, most important, do it again.

Never lose sight of your highest-priority interrupt.

In computing, a high-priority interrupt happens when something requires a computer processor's immediate attention, and the machine halts normal operations and jumps the urgent issue to the head of the processing queue. Like computer processors, team leaders have quite a few things that demand their attention and force them to act. Many of them are problems. If you see something go off the rails—a poorly handled call, a missed meeting, a project gone awry—the instinct will kick in to stop everything to tell someone what she did wrong and what she needs to do to fix it. This instinct is by no means misguided: If your team member screws something up, you have to deal with it. But remember that when you do, you're merely remediating—and that remediating not only inhibits learning but also gets you no closer to excellent performance. As we've seen, conjuring excellence from your team members requires a different focus from you. If you see somebody doing something that really works, stopping her and dissecting it with her isn't only a high-priority interrupt, it is your *highest*-priority interrupt. As you replay each small moment of excellence to your team member, you'll ease her into the "rest and digest" state of mind. Her understanding of what excellence looks and feels like within her will become more vivid, her brain will become more receptive to new information and will make connections to other inputs found in other regions of her brain, and she will learn and grow and get better.

Explore the present, past, and future.

When people come to you asking for feedback on their performance or what they might need to fix to get promoted, try this:

Start with the *present*. If a team member approaches you with a problem, he's dealing with it *now*. He's feeling weak or challenged, and you have to address that. But rather than tackling the problem head-on, ask your colleague to tell you three things that are working for him *right now*. These things might be related to the situation or entirely separate. They might be significant or trivial. Just ask the question, and you're priming him with oxytocin—which is sometimes called the "love drug" but which here is better thought of as the "creativity drug." Getting him to think about specific things that are going well will alter his brain chemistry so that he can be open to new solutions and new ways of thinking or acting.

Next, go to the *past*. Ask him, "When you had a problem like this in the past, what did you do that worked?" Much of our life happens in patterns, so it's highly likely that he has encountered this problem at least a few times before. On one of those occasions he will almost certainly have found some way forward, some action or insight or connection that enabled him to move out of the mess. Get him thinking about that and seeing it in his mind's eye: what he actually felt and did, and what happened next.

Finally, turn to the *future*. Ask your team member, "What do you already know you need to do? What do you already know works in this situation?" By all means offer up one or two of your own experiences to see if they might clarify his own. But operate under the assumption that he already knows the solution—you're just helping him recognize it.

The emphasis here should not be on whys—"Why didn't that work?" "Why do you think you should do that?"—because those lead both of you into a fuzzy world of conjecture and concepts. Instead, focus on the whats—"What do you actually want to have happen?" "What are a couple of actions you could take right now?" These sorts of questions yield concrete answers, in which your colleague can find his actual self doing actual things in the near-term future.

How to give people feedback is one of the hottest topics in business today. The arguments for radical candor and unvarnished and pervasive transparency have a swagger to them, almost as if to imply that only the finest and bravest of us can face these truths with nerveless self-assurance, that those of us who recoil at the thought of working in a climate of continual judgment are condemned to mediocrity, and that as leaders our ability to look our colleagues squarely in the eye and lay out their faults without blinking is a measure of our integrity.

But at best, this fetish with feedback is good only for correcting mistakes—in the rare cases where the right steps are known and can be evaluated objectively. And at worst, it's toxic, because what we want from our people—and from ourselves—is not, for the most part, tidy adherence to a procedure agreed upon in advance or, for that matter, the ability to expose one another's flaws. It's that people contribute their own unique and growing talents to a common good, when that good is ever-evolving, when we are, for all the right reasons, making it up as we go along. Feedback has nothing to offer to that.

We humans do not do well when someone whose intentions are unclear tells us where we stand, how good we "really" are, and what we must do to fix ourselves. We excel *only* when people who know us and care about us tell us what they experience and what they feel, and in particular when they see something within us that really works.

Originally published in March–April 2019. Reprint R1902G

The Authenticity Paradox

by Herminia Ibarra

AUTHENTICITY HAS BECOME THE GOLD standard for leadership. But a simplistic understanding of what it means can hinder your growth and limit your impact.

Consider Cynthia, a general manager in a health care organization. Her promotion into that role increased her direct reports 10-fold and expanded the range of businesses she oversaw—and she felt a little shaky about making such a big leap. A strong believer in transparent, collaborative leadership, she bared her soul to her new employees: "I want to do this job," she said, "but it's scary, and I need your help." Her candor backfired; she lost credibility with people who wanted and needed a confident leader to take charge.

Or take George, a Malaysian executive in an auto parts company where people valued a clear chain of command and made decisions by consensus. When a Dutch multinational with a matrix structure acquired the company, George found himself working with peers who saw decision-making as a freewheeling contest for the best-debated ideas. That style didn't come easily to him, and it contradicted everything he had learned about humility growing up in his country. In a 360-degree debrief, his boss told him that he needed to sell his ideas and accomplishments more aggressively. George felt he had to choose between being a failure and being a fake.

Because going against our natural inclinations can make us feel like impostors, we tend to latch on to authenticity as an excuse for sticking with what's comfortable. But few jobs allow us to do that for long. That's doubly true when we advance in our careers or when demands or expectations change, as Cynthia, George, and countless other executives have discovered.

In my research on leadership transitions, I have observed that career advances require all of us to move way beyond our comfort zones. At the same time, however, they trigger a strong countervailing impulse to protect our identities: When we are unsure of ourselves or our ability to perform well or measure up in a new setting, we often retreat to familiar behaviors and styles.

But my research also demonstrates that the moments that most challenge our sense of self are the ones that can teach us the most about leading effectively. By viewing ourselves as works in progress and evolving our professional identities through trial and error, we can develop a personal style that feels right to us and suits our organizations' changing needs.

That takes courage, because learning, by definition, starts with unnatural and often superficial behaviors that can make us feel calculating instead of genuine and spontaneous. But the only way to avoid being pigeonholed and ultimately become better leaders is to do the things that a rigidly authentic sense of self would keep us from doing.

Why Leaders Struggle with Authenticity

The word "authentic" traditionally referred to any work of art that is an original, not a copy. When used to describe leadership, of course, it has other meanings—and they can be problematic. For example, the notion of adhering to one "true self" flies in the face of much research on how people evolve with experience, discovering facets of themselves they would never have unearthed through introspection alone. And being utterly transparent—disclosing every single thought and feeling—is both unrealistic and risky.

Idea in Brief

The Problem

When we view authenticity as an unwavering sense of self, we struggle to take on new challenges and bigger roles. The reality is that people learn—and change—who they are through experience.

The Solution

By trying out different leadership styles and behaviors, we grow more than we would through introspection alone. Experimenting with our identities allows us to find the right approach for ourselves and our organizations.

The Sticking Point

This adaptive approach to authenticity can make us feel like impostors, because it involves doing things that may not come naturally. But it's outside our comfort zones that we learn the most about leading effectively.

Leaders today struggle with authenticity for several reasons. First, we make more-frequent and more-radical changes in the kinds of work we do. As we strive to *improve* our game, a clear and firm sense of self is a compass that helps us navigate choices and progress toward our goals. But when we're looking to *change* our game, a too rigid self-concept becomes an anchor that keeps us from sailing forth, as it did at first with Cynthia.

Second, in global business, many of us work with people who don't share our cultural norms and have different expectations for how we should behave. It can often seem as if we have to choose between what is expected—and therefore effective—and what feels authentic. George is a case in point.

Third, identities are always on display in today's world of ubiquitous connectivity and social media. How we present ourselves—not just as executives but as people, with quirks and broader interests—has become an important aspect of leadership. Having to carefully curate a persona that's out there for all to see can clash with our private sense of self.

In dozens of interviews with talented executives facing new expectations, I have found that they most often grapple with authenticity in the following situations.

Taking charge in an unfamiliar role.

As everyone knows, the first 90 days are critical in a new leadership role. First impressions form quickly, and they matter. Depending on their personalities, leaders respond very differently to the increased visibility and performance pressure.

Psychologist Mark Snyder, of the University of Minnesota, identified two psychological profiles that inform how leaders develop their personal styles. "High self-monitors"—or chameleons, as I call them—are naturally able and willing to adapt to the demands of a situation without feeling fake. Chameleons care about managing their public image and often mask their vulnerability with bluster. They may not always get it right the first time, but they keep trying on different styles like new clothes until they find a good fit for themselves and their circumstances. Because of that flexibility, they often advance rapidly. But chameleons can run into problems when people perceive them as disingenuous or lacking a moral center—even though they're expressing their "true" chameleon nature.

By contrast, "true-to-selfers" (Snyder's "low self-monitors") tend to express what they really think and feel, even when it runs counter to situational demands. The danger with true-to-selfers like Cynthia and George is that they may stick too long with comfortable behavior that prevents them from meeting new requirements, instead of evolving their style as they gain insight and experience.

Cynthia (whom I interviewed after her story appeared in a *Wall Street Journal* article by Carol Hymowitz) hemmed herself in like this. She thought she was setting herself up for success by staying true to her highly personal, full-disclosure style of management. She asked her new team for support, openly acknowledging that she felt a bit at sea. As she scrambled to learn unfamiliar aspects of the business, she worked tirelessly to contribute to every decision and solve every problem. After a few months, she was on the verge of burnout. To make matters worse, sharing her vulnerability with her team members so early on had damaged her standing. Reflecting on her transition some years later, Cynthia told me: "Being authentic doesn't mean that you can be held up to the light and people can see right through you." But at the time, that was how she saw it—and instead of building trust, she made people question her ability to do the job.

Delegating and communicating appropriately are only part of the problem in a case like this. A deeper-seated issue is finding the right mix of distance and closeness in an unfamiliar situation. Stanford psychologist Deborah Gruenfeld describes this as managing the tension between authority and approachability. To be authoritative, you privilege your knowledge, experience, and expertise over the team's, maintaining a measure of distance. To be approachable, you emphasize your relationships with people, their input, and their perspective, and you lead with empathy and warmth. Getting the balance right presents an acute authenticity crisis for true-to-selfers, who typically have a strong preference for behaving one way or the other. Cynthia made herself too approachable and vulnerable, and it undermined and drained her. In her bigger role, she needed more distance from her employees to gain their confidence and get the job done.

Selling your ideas (and yourself).

Leadership growth usually involves a shift from having good ideas to pitching them to diverse stakeholders. Inexperienced leaders, especially true-to-selfers, often find the process of getting buy-in distasteful because it feels artificial and political; they believe that their work should stand on its own merits.

Here's an example: Anne, a senior manager at a transportation company, had doubled revenue and fundamentally redesigned core processes in her unit. Despite her obvious accomplishments, however, her boss didn't consider her an inspirational leader. Anne also knew she was not communicating effectively in her role as a board member of the parent company. The chairman, a broad-brush thinker, often became impatient with her detail orientation. His feedback to her was "step up, do the vision thing." But to Anne that seemed like valuing form over substance. "For me, it is manipulation," she told me in an interview. "I can do the storytelling too, but I refuse to play on people's emotions. If the string-pulling is too obvious, I can't make myself do it." Like many aspiring leaders, she resisted crafting emotional messages to influence and inspire others because that felt less authentic to her than relying on facts, figures, and spreadsheets. As a result, she worked at cross-purposes with the board chairman, pushing hard on the facts instead of pulling him in as a valued ally.

Many managers know deep down that their good ideas and strong potential will go unnoticed if they don't do a better job of selling themselves. Still, they can't bring themselves to do it. "I try to build a network based on professionalism and what I can deliver for the business, not who I know," one manager told me. "Maybe that's not smart from a career point of view. But I can't go against my beliefs. . . . So I have been more limited in 'networking up.'"

Until we see career advancement as a way of extending our reach and increasing our impact in the organization—a collective win, not just a selfish pursuit—we have trouble feeling authentic when touting our strengths to influential people. True-to-selfers find it particularly hard to sell themselves to senior management when they most need to do so: when they are still unproven. Research shows, however, that this hesitancy disappears as people gain experience and become more certain of the value they bring.

Processing negative feedback.

Many successful executives encounter serious negative feedback for the first time in their careers when they take on larger roles or responsibilities. Even when the criticisms aren't exactly new, they loom larger because the stakes are higher. But leaders often convince themselves that dysfunctional aspects of their "natural" style are the inevitable price of being effective.

Let's look at Jacob, a food company production manager whose direct reports gave him low marks in a 360 review on emotional intelligence, team building, and empowering others. One team member wrote that it was hard for Jacob to accept criticism. Another remarked that after an angry outburst, he'd suddenly make a joke as if nothing had happened, not realizing the destabilizing effect of his mood

Why Companies Are Pushing Authenticity Training

MANAGERS CAN CHOOSE from countless books, articles, and executive workshops for advice on how to be more authentic at work. Two trends help explain the exploding popularity of the concept and the training industry it has fed.

First, trust in business leaders fell to an all-time low in 2012, according to the Edelman Trust Barometer. Even in 2013, when trust began to climb back up, only 18% of people reported that they trusted business leaders to tell the truth, and fewer than half trusted businesses to do the right thing.

Second, employee engagement is at a nadir. A 2013 Gallup poll found that only 13% of employees worldwide are engaged at work. Only one in eight workers—out of roughly 180 million employees studied—is psychologically committed to his or her job. In study after study, frustration, burnout, disillusionment, and misalignment with personal values are cited among the biggest reasons for career change.

At a time when public confidence and employee morale are so low, it's no surprise that companies are encouraging leaders to discover their "true" selves.

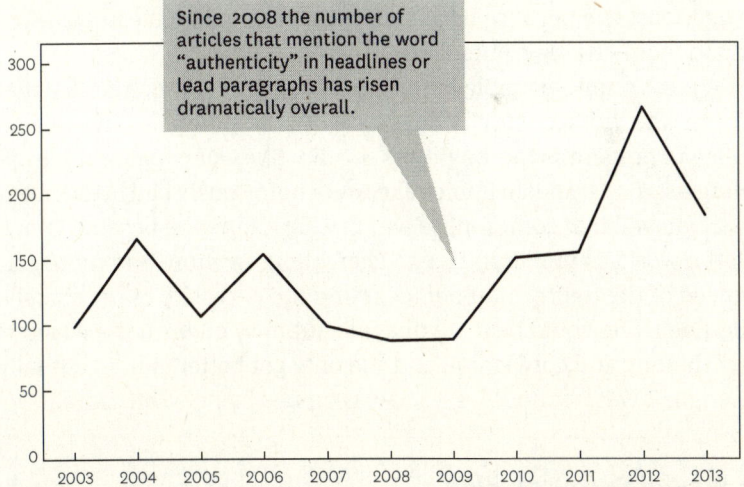

Since 2008 the number of articles that mention the word "authenticity" in headlines or lead paragraphs has risen dramatically overall.

Source: *New York Times, Financial Times, Washington Post, Economist, Forbes, Wall Street Journal,* and *HBR*

changes on those around him. For someone who genuinely believed that he'd built trust among his people, all this was tough to swallow.

Once the initial shock had subsided, Jacob acknowledged that this was not the first time he'd received such criticism (some colleagues and subordinates had made similar comments a few years earlier). "I thought I'd changed my approach," he reflected, "but I haven't really changed so much since the last time." However, he quickly rationalized his behavior to his boss: "Sometimes you have to be tough in order to deliver results, and people don't like it," he said. "You have to accept that as part of the job description." Of course, he was missing the point.

Because negative feedback given to leaders often centers on style rather than skills or expertise, it can feel like a threat to their identity—as if they're being asked to give up their "secret sauce." That's how Jacob saw it. Yes, he could be explosive—but from his point of view, his "toughness" allowed him to deliver results year after year. In reality, though, he had succeeded up to this point *despite* his behavior. When his role expanded and he took on greater responsibility, his intense scrutiny of subordinates became an even bigger obstacle because it took up time he should have been devoting to more-strategic pursuits.

A great public example of this phenomenon is Margaret Thatcher. Those who worked with her knew she could be merciless if someone failed to prepare as thoroughly as she did. She was capable of humiliating a staff member in public, she was a notoriously bad listener, and she believed that compromise was cowardice. As she became known to the world as the "Iron Lady," Thatcher grew more and more convinced of the rightness of her ideas and the necessity of her coercive methods. She could beat anyone into submission with the power of her rhetoric and conviction, and she only got better at it. Eventually, though, it was her undoing—she was ousted by her own cabinet.

A Playful Frame of Mind

Such a rigid self-concept can result from too much introspection. When we look only within for answers, we inadvertently reinforce old ways of seeing the world and outdated views of ourselves.

Without the benefit of what I call outsight—the valuable external perspective we get from experimenting with new leadership behaviors—habitual patterns of thought and action fence us in. To begin thinking like leaders, we must first act: plunge ourselves into new projects and activities, interact with very different kinds of people, and experiment with new ways of getting things done. Especially in times of transition and uncertainty, thinking and introspection should follow experience—not vice versa. Action changes who we are and what we believe is worth doing.

Fortunately, there are ways of increasing outsight and evolving toward an "adaptively authentic" way of leading, but they require a playful frame of mind. Think of leadership development as trying on possible selves rather than working on yourself—which, let's face it, sounds like drudgery. When we adopt a playful attitude, we're more open to possibilities. It's OK to be inconsistent from one day to the next. That's not being a fake; it's how we experiment to figure out what's right for the new challenges and circumstances we face.

My research suggests three important ways to get started.

Learn from diverse role models.

Most learning necessarily involves some form of imitation—and the understanding that nothing is "original." An important part of growing as a leader is viewing authenticity not as an intrinsic state but as the ability to take elements you have learned from others' styles and behaviors and make them your own.

But don't copy just one person's leadership style; tap many diverse role models. There is a big difference between imitating someone wholesale and borrowing selectively from various people to create your own collage, which you then modify and improve. As the playwright Wilson Mizner said, copying one author is plagiarism, but copying many is research.

I observed the importance of this approach in a study of investment bankers and consultants who were advancing from analytical and project work to roles advising clients and selling new business. Though most of them felt incompetent and insecure in their new positions, the chameleons among them consciously borrowed styles and tactics from successful senior leaders—learning through emulation how to use humor to break tension in meetings, for instance, and how to shape opinion without being overbearing. Essentially, the chameleons faked it until they found what worked for them. Noticing their efforts, their managers provided coaching and mentoring and shared tacit knowledge.

As a result, the chameleons arrived much faster at an authentic but more skillful style than the true-to-selfers in the study, who continued to focus solely on demonstrating technical mastery. Often the true-to-selfers concluded that their managers were "all talk and little content" and therefore not suitable role models. In the absence of a "perfect" model they had a harder time with imitation—it felt bogus. Unfortunately, their managers perceived their inability to adapt as a lack of effort or investment and thus didn't give them as much mentoring and coaching as they gave the chameleons.

Work on getting better.
Setting goals for learning (not just for performance) helps us experiment with our identities without feeling like impostors, because we don't expect to get everything right from the start. We stop trying to protect our comfortable old selves from the threats that change can bring, and start exploring what kinds of leaders we might become.

Of course, we all want to perform well in a new situation—get the right strategy in place, execute like crazy, deliver results the organization cares about. But focusing exclusively on those things makes us afraid to take risks in the service of learning. In a series of ingenious experiments, Stanford psychologist Carol Dweck has shown that concern about how we will appear to others inhibits learning on new or unfamiliar tasks. Performance goals motivate us to show others that we possess valued attributes, such as intelligence and social skill, and to prove to ourselves that we have them. By contrast, learning goals motivate us to develop valued attributes.

The Cultural Factor

WHATEVER THE SITUATION—TAKING charge in unfamiliar territory, selling your ideas and yourself, or processing negative feedback—finding authentic ways of being effective is even more difficult in a multicultural environment.

As my INSEAD colleague Erin Meyer finds in her research, styles of persuading others and the kinds of arguments that people find persuasive are far from universal; they are deeply rooted in a culture's philosophical, religious, and educational assumptions. That said, prescriptions for how leaders are supposed to look and sound are rarely as diverse as the leaders themselves. And despite corporate initiatives to build understanding of cultural differences and promote diversity, the fact is that leaders are still expected to express ideas assertively, to claim credit for them, and to use charisma to motivate and inspire people.

Authenticity is supposed to be an antidote to a single model of leadership. (After all, the message is to be yourself, not what someone else expects you to be.) But as the notion has gained currency, it has, ironically, come to mean something much more limiting and culturally specific. A closer look at how leaders are taught to discover and demonstrate authenticity—by telling a personal story about a hardship they have overcome, for example—reveals a model that is, in fact, very American, based on ideals such as self-disclosure, humility, and individualistic triumph over adversity.

This amounts to a catch-22 for managers from cultures with different norms for authority, communication, and collective endeavor because they must behave inauthentically in order to conform to the strictures of "authentic" leadership.

When we're in performance mode, leadership is about presenting ourselves in the most favorable light. In learning mode, we can reconcile our yearning for authenticity in how we work and lead with an equally powerful desire to grow. One leader I met was highly effective in small-group settings but struggled to convey openness to new ideas in larger meetings, where he often stuck to long-winded presentations for fear of getting derailed by others' comments. He set himself a "no PowerPoint" rule to develop a more relaxed, improvisational style. He surprised himself by how much he learned, not only about his own evolving preferences but also about the issues at hand.

Don't stick to "your story."

Most of us have personal narratives about defining moments that taught us important lessons. Consciously or not, we allow our stories, and the images of ourselves that they paint, to guide us in new situations. But the stories can become outdated as we grow, so sometimes it's necessary to alter them dramatically or even to throw them out and start from scratch.

That was true for Maria, a leader who saw herself as a "mother hen with her chicks all around." Her coach, former Ogilvy & Mather CEO Charlotte Beers, explains in *I'd Rather Be in Charge* that this self-image emerged from a time when Maria had to sacrifice her own goals and dreams to take care of her extended family. It eventually began to hold her back in her career: Though it had worked for her as a friendly and loyal team player and a peacekeeper, it wasn't helping her get the big leadership assignment she wanted. Together Maria and her coach looked for another defining moment to use as a touchstone—one that was more in keeping with Maria's desired future self, not who she had been in the past. They chose the time when Maria, as a young woman, had left her family to travel the world for 18 months. Acting from that bolder sense of self, she asked for—and got—a promotion that had previously been elusive.

Dan McAdams, a Northwestern psychology professor who has spent his career studying life stories, describes identity as "the internalized and evolving story that results from a person's selective appropriation of past, present and future." This isn't just academic jargon. McAdams is saying that you have to believe your story—but also embrace how it changes over time, according to what you need it to do. Try out new stories about yourself, and keep editing them, much as you would your résumé.

Again, revising one's story is both an introspective and a social process. The narratives we choose should not only sum up our experiences and aspirations but also reflect the demands we face and resonate with the audience we're trying to win over.

Countless books and advisers tell you to start your leadership journey with a clear sense of who you are. But that can be a recipe for staying stuck in the past. Your leadership identity can and should change each time you move on to bigger and better things.

The only way we grow as leaders is by stretching the limits of who we are—doing new things that make us uncomfortable but that teach us through direct experience who we want to become. Such growth doesn't require a radical personality makeover. Small changes—in the way we carry ourselves, the way we communicate, the way we interact—often make a world of difference in how effectively we lead.

Originally published in January–February 2015. Reprint R1501C

The C-Suite Skills That Matter Most

by Raffaella Sadun, Joseph Fuller, Stephen Hansen, and PJ Neal

FOR A LONG TIME, whenever companies wanted to hire a CEO or another key executive, they knew what to look for: somebody with technical expertise, superior administrative skills, and a track record of successfully managing financial resources. When courting outside candidates to fill those roles, they often favored executives from companies such as GE, IBM, and P&G and from professional-services giants such as McKinsey and Deloitte, which had a reputation for cultivating those skills in their managers.

That practice now feels like ancient history. So much has changed during the past two decades that companies can no longer assume that leaders with traditional managerial pedigrees will succeed in the C-suite. Today firms need to hire executives who are able to motivate diverse, technologically savvy, and global workforces; who can play the role of corporate statesperson, dealing effectively with constituents ranging from sovereign governments to influential NGOs; and who can rapidly and effectively apply their skills in a new company, in what may be an unfamiliar industry, and often with colleagues in the C-suite whom they didn't previously know.

These changes present a phenomenal challenge for executive recruitment, because the capabilities required of top leaders include new and often "softer" skills that are rarely explicitly recognized or fostered in the corporate world. Simply put, it's getting harder and less prudent to rely on traditional indicators of managerial potential.

What should organizations do to face this challenge? A critical first step is to develop greater clarity about what it now takes for C-suite executives to succeed. Yes, the range of necessary skills appears to have expanded—but how exactly? For example, what does the term "soft skills" really mean? And to what extent does the need to hire executives with more-expansive skills vary across organizations?

Remarkably, even though almost every aspect of leadership has been scrutinized in recent years, rigorous evidence on these crucial points is scant. To find out more—about the capabilities that are now in demand, how those have changed over time, and what adjustments companies are making to their process for selecting candidates—we recently analyzed data from Russell Reynolds Associates, one of the world's premier executive-search firms. Russell Reynolds and its competitors play an essential role in managerial labor markets: 80% to 90% of the *Fortune* 250 and FTSE 100 companies use the services of such firms when making a succession decision that involves a choice among candidates. (Disclosure: Russell Reynolds has recently conducted executive searches for Harvard Business Publishing, which publishes *Harvard Business Review*.)

For our research, Russell Reynolds gave us unprecedented access to nearly 5,000 job descriptions that it had developed in collaboration with its clients from 2000 to 2017. The data was sufficient to study expectations not just for the CEO but also for four other key leaders in the C-suite: the chief financial officer, the chief information officer, the head of human resources, and the chief marketing officer. To our knowledge, researchers had never before analyzed such a comprehensive collection of senior-executive job descriptions. (For more about how we worked with the data, see the sidebar "About the Research.")

Our study yielded a variety of insights. Chief among them is this: Over the past two decades, companies have significantly redefined

Idea in Brief

The Shift

It's no longer safe to assume that leaders with traditional managerial pedigrees will succeed in the C-suite. An analysis of executive-search data shows that companies today are prioritizing social skills above technical know-how, expertise in financial stewardship, and other qualifications.

The Explanation

Large companies today have increasingly complex operations, heavier reliance on technology, more workforce diversity, and greater public accountability for their behavior. Leading under those circumstances requires superior listening and communication skills and an ability to relate well to multiple constituencies.

The Path Forward

To succeed in the years ahead, companies will have to figure out how to effectively evaluate the social skills of job candidates. They will also need to make such skills an integral part of their talent-management strategies.

the roles of C-suite executives. The traditional capabilities mentioned earlier—notably the management of financial and operational resources—remain highly relevant. But when companies today search for top leaders, especially new CEOs, they attribute less importance to those capabilities than they used to and instead prioritize one qualification above all others: strong social skills. (See the exhibit "Help wanted: CEOs who are good with people.")

When we refer to "social skills," we mean certain specific capabilities, including a high level of self-awareness, the ability to listen and communicate well, a facility for working with different types of people and groups, and what psychologists call "theory of mind"—the capacity to infer how others are thinking and feeling. The magnitude of the shift in recent years toward these capabilities is most significant for CEOs but also pronounced for the four other C-suite roles we studied.

Our analysis revealed that social skills are particularly important in settings where productivity hinges on effective communication, as it invariably does in the large, complex, and skill-intensive enterprises

About the Research

THIS ARTICLE IS BASED ON a rich data set drawn from almost 5,000 job descriptions compiled by Russell Reynolds Associates and companies conducting searches for various C-suite positions. Translating that data into variables that were amenable to quantitative analysis was no easy feat, because the job descriptions did not follow a standard structure or contain standard content. Our approach involved two steps.

First we defined a distinctive set of skill requirements that were relevant for chief executives. We started by combing through the U.S. Department of Labor's O*NET database (a repository of information about more than 1,000 occupations) to see what skills were listed for "chief executive" roles. We then sorted those into six clusters that included similar tasks: managing financial and material resources; monitoring corporate performance; tending to human resources; handling administrative tasks; processing and using complex information; and exercising social skills.

Our second step was to determine the extent to which each job description provided by Russell Reynolds was semantically similar to each O*NET skills cluster.

Both steps relied on a model of managerial language that we developed by applying cutting-edge machine-learning techniques (word2vec) to a corpus composed of every *Harvard Business Review* article published since the magazine's inception in 1922.

that employ executive search firms. In such organizations, CEOs and other senior leaders can't limit themselves to performing routine operational tasks. They also have to spend a significant amount of time interacting with others and enabling coordination—by communicating information, facilitating the exchange of ideas, building and overseeing teams, and identifying and solving problems.

Intriguingly, the evolution of skills requirements in the C-suite parallels developments in the workforce as a whole. At all employment levels today, more and more jobs require highly developed social skills. Harvard's David Deming, among others, has demonstrated that such jobs have grown at a faster rate than the labor market as a whole—and that compensation for them is growing faster than average.

Help wanted: CEOs who are good with people

Since 2007, companies advertising C-suite openings have increasingly emphasized the importance of social skills and deemphasized operational expertise.

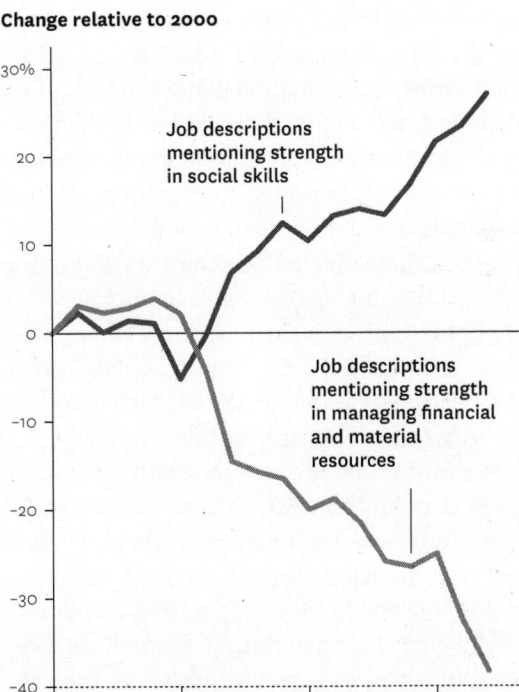

Change relative to 2000

Job descriptions mentioning strength in social skills

Job descriptions mentioning strength in managing financial and material resources

Note: Job descriptions were for nearly 5,000 C-suite positions advertised by the executive-search firm Russell Reynolds Associates. The data points were estimated in a regression model that controls for industry differences and other variables. The coefficients after 2007 are significantly different from zero across both skill clusters.

Why is this shift toward social skills taking place? And what implications does it have for executive development, CEO succession planning, and the organization of the C-suite? This article offers some preliminary thoughts.

The Chief Reasons for Change

We've identified two main drivers of the growing demand for social skills.

Firm size and complexity.

The focus on social skills is especially evident in large firms. Additionally, among firms of similar size, the demand for social skills is greater at publicly listed multinational enterprises and those that are involved in mergers and acquisitions. These patterns are consistent with the view that in larger and more complex organizations, top managers are increasingly expected to coordinate disparate and specialized knowledge, match the organization's problems with people who can solve them, and effectively orchestrate internal communication. For all those tasks, it helps to be able to interact well with others.

But the importance of social skills in large companies arises from more than just the complexity of operations there. It also reflects the web of critical relationships that leaders at such firms must cultivate and maintain with outside constituencies.

The diversity and number of those relationships can be daunting. Executives at public companies have to worry not only about product markets but also about capital markets. They need to brief analysts, woo asset managers, and address the business press. They must respond to various kinds of regulators across multiple jurisdictions. They're expected to communicate well with key customers and suppliers. During mergers and acquisitions, they have to attend carefully to constituents who are important to closing the transaction and supporting the post-merger integration. Highly developed social skills are critical to success in all those arenas.

Information-processing technologies.

"The more we automate information handling," management guru Peter Drucker wrote several decades ago, "the more we will have to create opportunities for effective communication." That has turned out to be prescient: Companies that rely significantly on information-processing technologies today also tend to be those that need leaders with especially strong social skills.

Here's why. Increasingly, in every part of the organization, when companies automate routine tasks, their competitiveness hinges on capabilities that computer systems simply don't have—things such as judgment, creativity, and perception. In technologically intensive firms, where automation is widespread, leaders have to align a heterogeneous workforce, respond to unexpected events, and manage conflict in the decision-making process, all of which are best done by managers with strong social skills.

Moreover, most companies today rely on many of the same technological platforms—Amazon Web Services, Facebook, Google, Microsoft, Salesforce, Workday. That means they have less opportunity to differentiate themselves on the basis of tangible technological investments alone. When every major competitor in a market leverages the same suite of tools, leaders need to distinguish themselves through superior management of the people who use those tools. That requires them to be top-notch communicators in every regard, able both to devise the right messages and to deliver them with empathy.

In sum, as more tasks are entrusted to technology, workers with superior social skills will be in demand at all levels and will command a premium in the labor market.

Other Factors

Our research suggests that the growing interest in social skills is being spurred by two additional drivers. These are harder to quantify, but they nonetheless may play an important role in the shift that's taking place.

Social media and networking technologies.
Historically, CEOs didn't attract much popular notice, nor did they seek the limelight. While other businesspeople, investors, and members of the business press paid attention to them, the public generally did not, except in the cases of "celebrity" CEOs such as GE's Jack Welch, Sony's Akio Morita, and Chrysler's Lee Iacocca.

That era is over. As companies move away from shareholder primacy and focus more broadly on stakeholder capitalism, CEOs and other senior leaders are expected to be public figures. They're obliged not only to interact with an increasingly broad range of internal and external constituencies but to do so personally and transparently and accountably. No longer can they rely on support functions—the corporate communications team, the government relations department, and so forth—to take care of all those relationships.

Furthermore, top leaders must manage interactions in real time, thanks to the increasing prevalence of both social media (which can capture and publicize missteps nearly instantaneously) and network platforms such as Slack and Glassdoor (which allow employees to widely disseminate information and opinions about their colleagues and bosses).

In the past, too, executives were expected to be able to explain and defend everything from their business strategies to their HR practices. But they did so in a controlled environment, at a time and a place of management's choosing. Now they must be constantly attuned to how their decisions are perceived by various audiences. Failing to achieve their intended purposes with even a handful of employees or other constituents can be damaging.

So social skills matter greatly. The occupants of the C-suite need to be adroit at communicating spontaneously and anticipating how their words and actions will play beyond the immediate context.

Diversity and inclusion.
Another new challenge for CEOs and other senior leaders is dealing with issues of diversity and inclusion—publicly, empathetically, and proactively. That, too, demands strong social skills, particularly theory of mind. Executives who possess that perceptiveness about the mental states of others can move more easily among various employee groups, make them feel heard, and represent their interests within the organization, to the board of directors, and to outside constituencies. More importantly, they can nurture an environment in which diverse talent thrives.

New Areas for Focus

Given the critical role that social skills play in leadership success today, companies will need to refocus on the following areas as they hire and cultivate new leaders.

Systematically building social skills.

Traditionally, boards and senior executives have cultivated future leaders by rotating them through critical departments and functions, posting them to various geographic locations, and putting them through executive development programs. It was assumed that the best way to prepare promising managers for a future in the C-suite was to have them develop deep competence in a variety of administrative and operational roles.

With this model, evaluating success and failure was reasonably straightforward. Processes ran smoothly or they didn't; results were achieved or they weren't. Social skills mattered, of course: As up-and-comers moved through functions and geographies, their ability to quickly form constructive relationships with colleagues, customers, regulators, and suppliers affected their performance. But such skills were considered something of a bonus. They were a means to achieving operational objectives (a prerequisite for advancement) and were seldom evaluated in an explicit, systematic, and objective way.

Companies today better appreciate the importance of social skills in executive performance, but they've made little progress in devising processes for evaluating a candidate's proficiency in those skills and determining aptitude for further growth. Few companies invest in training to improve the interviewing skills of staffers involved in recruiting—least of all senior executives or independent directors, who are presumed to have the background and perspective necessary to make sound judgments.

Getting references is also problematic: Companies typically conduct senior-level searches with a high degree of confidentiality, both to protect themselves (a leak could cost them the best prospect) and to protect the candidates (who might not want their employers to know that they're open to job offers). Moreover, the people conducting C-suite interviews and those providing references are likely to be part of the same small, homogeneous networks as most of the candidates, which significantly heightens the risk of bias in the decision-making process. For example, board members tend to support candidates who are referred by friends or have backgrounds similar to their own. They might mistakenly assume that those individuals possess broadly applicable social skills simply because they connected easily with them in interviews.

To better evaluate social skills, some companies now run psychometric assessments or simulations. Psychometric tests (which are designed to measure personality traits and behavioral style) can help establish whether someone is outgoing and comfortable with strangers, but they shed little light on how effective that person will be when interacting with various groups. Simulation exercises, for their part, have been used for some time to evaluate how individuals respond to challenging circumstances, but they're usually designed around a specific scenario, such as a product-integrity crisis or the arrival of an activist investor on the scene. Simulations are best at assessing candidates' administrative and technical skills in such situations, rather than their ability to coordinate teams or interact spontaneously with diverse constituencies. Even so, these exercises are not widely used, because of the time and money required to run them well.

In their executive development programs, companies today need a systematic approach to building and evaluating social skills. They may even need to prioritize them over the "hard" skills that managers presently favor because they're so easy to assess. Companies should place high-potential leaders in positions that oblige them to interact with various employee populations and external constituencies and then closely monitor their performance in those roles.

Assessing social skills innovatively.

The criteria that companies have traditionally used to size up candidates for C-suite positions—such as work history, technical qualifications, and career trajectory—are of limited value in assessing social skills. Companies will need to create new tools if they are to establish an objective basis for evaluating and comparing people's abilities in this realm. They can act either independently or in conjunction with the professional-services firms that support them, but in either case they'll need to custom-design solutions to serve their particular needs.

Although appropriate tools have yet to be developed for searches at the highest echelons of organizations, considerable innovation is underway when it comes to ascertaining the skills of lower-level job seekers and placing them in the right positions. Companies such as Eightfold and Gloat, for example, are using artificial intelligence to improve matching between candidates and employers. New custom tools are also being used to identify skill adjacencies and to create internal talent marketplaces, helping companies assign qualified employees to important tasks more quickly. The underlying algorithms rely on huge data sets, which poses a technological challenge, but this approach holds promise for executive recruiting.

Similarly, pymetrics, among other companies, is mining world-class behavioral research to see how particular candidates fit with an organization or a specific position. Such an approach has proved useful in evaluating a broad array of soft skills and in reducing bias in recruiting. Recent academic work shows the utility of tapping into behavioral research: Harvard's Ben Weidmann and David Deming, for example, have found that the Reading the Mind in the Eyes Test, a well-established measure of social intelligence, can effectively predict the performance of individuals in team settings. If companies develop new tests based on the same design principles, they and their boards of directors should be able to gain a fuller and more objective understanding of the social skills of C-suite candidates.

Emphasizing social skills development at all levels.
Companies that rely on outside hiring to find executives with superior social skills are playing a dangerous game. For one thing, competition for such people will become fierce. For another, it's inherently risky to put an outsider—even someone carefully vetted—in a senior

role. Companies thus will benefit from a "grow your own" approach that allows internal up-and-comers to hone and demonstrate a range of interpersonal abilities.

Assessing the collective social skills in the C-suite.
Increasingly, boards of directors and company executives will need to develop and evaluate the social skills of not only individual leaders but the C-suite as a whole. Weakness or ineptitude on the part of any one person on the team will have a systems effect on the group— and especially the CEO. Companies recognize this: Social skills are gaining in relative importance in the search criteria for all five of the executive positions we studied. Moreover, as CEOs continue playing a bigger role in constituency and personnel management, the responsibilities within the C-suite may be reconfigured, and other executives will need strong social skills too.

The Way Forward

As we've established, companies still value C-suite executives with traditional administrative and operational skills. But they're increasingly on the lookout for people with highly developed social skills—especially if their organizations are large, complex, and technologically intensive.

Will companies, however, actually succeed in making different kinds of hires? That's an open question. The answer will depend in part on whether they can figure out how to effectively evaluate the social skills of job candidates, and whether they decide to make the cultivation of social skills an integral component of their talent-management strategies.

In our view, companies are going to have to do both those things to remain competitive. To that end, they should encourage business schools and other educators to place more emphasis on social skills in their MBA and executive-level curricula, and they should challenge search firms and other intermediaries to devise innovative mechanisms for identifying and assessing candidates.

Companies themselves will also have to do things differently. In recruiting and evaluating outside talent, they must prioritize social skills. The same is true when it comes to measuring the performance of current executives and setting their compensation. In addition, firms should make strong social skills a criterion for promotion, and they should task supervisors with nurturing such skills in high-potential subordinates.

In the years ahead, some companies may focus on trying to better identify and hire leaders with "the right stuff"; others may pay more attention to executive training and retention. But no matter what approach they adopt, it's clear that to succeed in an increasingly challenging business environment, they'll have to profoundly rethink their current practices.

Originally published in July–August 2022. Reprint S22041

Building an Ethical Career

A three-stage approach to navigating moral challenges at work. *by Maryam Kouchaki and Isaac H. Smith*

MOST OF US THINK of ourselves as good people. We set out to be ethical, and we hope that in pivotal moments we will rise to the occasion. But when it comes to building an ethical career, good intentions are insufficient. Decades' worth of research has identified social and psychological processes and biases that cloud people's moral judgment, leading them to violate their own values and often to create contorted, post hoc justifications for their behavior. So how can you ensure that from day to day and decade to decade you will do the right thing in your professional life?

The first step requires shifting to a mindset we term *moral humility*—the recognition that we all have the capacity to transgress if we're not vigilant. Moral humility pushes people to admit that temptations, rationalizations, and situations can lead even the best of us to misbehave, and it encourages them to think of ethics as not only avoiding the bad but also pursuing the good. It helps them see this sort of character development as a lifelong pursuit. We've been conducting research on morality and ethics in the workplace for more than a decade, and on the basis of our own and others' findings, we suggest that people who want to develop ethical careers should consider a three-stage approach: (1) Prepare in advance for moral challenges; (2) make good decisions in the moment; and (3) reflect on and learn from moral successes and failures.

Planning to be Good

Preparing for ethical challenges is important, because people are often well aware of what they *should* do when thinking about the future but tend to focus on what they *want* to do in the present. This tendency to overestimate the virtuousness of our future selves is part of what Ann Tenbrunsel of Notre Dame and colleagues call *the ethical mirage.*

Counteracting this bias begins with understanding your personal strengths and weaknesses. What are your values? When are you most likely to violate them? In his book *The Road to Character*, David Brooks distinguishes between *résumé* virtues (skills, abilities, and accomplishments that you can put on your résumé, such as "increased ROI by 10% on a multimillion-dollar project") and *eulogy* virtues (things people praise you for after you've died, such as being a loyal friend, kind, and a hard worker). Although the two categories may overlap, résumé virtues often relate to what you've done for yourself, whereas eulogy virtues relate to the person you are and what you've done for others—that is, your character.

So ask yourself: What eulogy virtues am I trying to develop? Or, as the management guru Peter Drucker asked, "What do you want to be remembered for?" and "What do you want to contribute?" Framing your professional life as a quest for contribution rather than achievement can fundamentally change the way you approach your career. And it's helpful to consider those questions early, before you develop mindsets, habits, and routines that are resistant to change.

Goal setting can also lay the groundwork for ethical behavior. Professionals regularly set targets for many aspects of their work and personal lives, yet few think to approach ethics in this way. Benjamin Franklin famously wrote in his autobiography about trying to master 13 traits he identified as essential for a virtuous life (including industry, justice, and humility). He even created a chart to track his daily progress. We don't suggest that everyone engage in

Idea in Brief

The Problem

Most of us think of ourselves as good people. We set out to be ethical at work, and we hope that in pivotal moments we will rise to the occasion. But when it comes to building an ethical career, good intentions are insufficient. Decades' worth of research has identified psychological processes and biases that cloud people's moral judgment, leading them to violate their own values, and often to create contorted, post hoc justifications for their behavior.

The Solution

How can we ensure that we will consistently do the right thing in our professional lives? It is necessary to shift mindset to *moral humility*—the recognition that we all have the capacity for ethical transgressions if we aren't vigilant. There is an effective three-stage approach for staying on the straight and narrow: Prepare in advance for moral challenges, including instituting proper safeguards; make good decisions in the moment; and reflect on and learn from moral successes and failures.

similarly rigid documentation, but we do suggest that you sit down and write out eulogy-virtue goals that are challenging but attainable. That is similar to what Clayton Christensen of Harvard Business School advocated in his HBR article "How Will You Measure Your Life?" After battling cancer, Christensen decided that the metric that mattered most to him was "the individual people whose lives I've touched."

Even the most carefully constructed goals, however, are still just good intentions. They must be fortified by personal safeguards—that is, habits and tendencies that have been shown to bring out people's better angels. For instance, studies suggest that quality sleep, personal prayer (for the religious), and mindfulness can help people manage and strengthen their self-control and resist temptation at work.

We also recommend "if-then planning"—what the psychologist Peter Gollwitzer calls *implementation intentions*. Dozens of research studies have shown that this practice ("If X happens, then I will do Y") can be effective in changing people's behavior, especially when such plans are voiced aloud. They can be simple but must also be specific, tying a situational cue (a trigger) to a desired behavior.

For example: *If* my boss asks me to do something potentially unethical, *then* I will turn to a friend or a mentor outside the organization for advice before acting. *If* I am solicited for a bribe, *then* I will consult my company's legal team and formal policies for guidance. *If* I witness sexual harassment or racial prejudice, *then* I will immediately stand up for the victim. Making if-then plans tailored to your strengths, weaknesses, values, and circumstances can help protect you against lapses in self-control, or inaction when action is required. But be sure to make your if-then plans *before* you encounter the situation—preparation is key.

Mentors, too, can help you avoid ethical missteps. When expanding your professional network and developing relationships with advisers, don't look only for those who can hasten your climb up the career ladder; also consider who might be able to support you when it comes to moral decisions. Build connections with people inside and outside your organization whose values are similar to yours and whom you can ask for ethics-related advice. Both of us have reached out to mentors for advice on ethical issues, and we teach our MBA students to do the same. Having a supportive network—and particularly a trusted ethical mentor—may also bring you opportunities to make a positive impact in your career.

Once you've made a commitment to living an ethical life, don't be shy about letting people know it. No one likes a holier-than-thou attitude, but subtle moral signaling can be helpful, particularly when it's directed at colleagues. You can do this by openly discussing potential moral challenges and how you would want to react or by building a reputation for doing things the right way. For example, in a study one of us (Maryam) conducted, participants were much less likely to ask an online partner to engage in unethical behavior after receiving an email from that partner with a virtuous quotation in the signature line (such as "Success without honor is worse than fraud").

Direct conversation can be tricky, given that people are often hesitant to discuss ethically charged issues. But if you think it's possible, we recommend engaging your coworkers, because ambiguity is a breeding ground for self-interested rationalization. Tactfully ask clarifying questions and make your own expectations clear: for example, "I think it's important that we don't cross any ethical lines here."

We are all shaped more by our environment than we realize, so it's also critical to choose a workplace that will allow if not encourage you to behave ethically. Not surprisingly, employees who feel that their needs, abilities, and values fit well with their organization tend to be more satisfied and motivated than their misaligned peers, and they perform better. Of course, many factors go into choosing a job—but in general people tend to overemphasize traditional metrics such as compensation and promotion opportunities and underemphasize the importance of the right *moral* fit. Our work and that of others has shown that ethical stress is a strong predictor of employee fatigue, decreased job satisfaction, lower motivation, and increased turnover.

Some industries seem to have cultural norms that are more or less amenable to dishonesty. In one study, when employees of a large international bank were reminded of their professional identity, they tended to cheat more, on average, than non-banker counterparts given the same reminder. This is not to say, of course, that all bankers are unethical, or that only unethical people should pursue careers in banking (although it does highlight how important it is for banks to prioritize hiring morally upstanding employees). We do suggest, however, that anyone starting a new job should learn about the organization and the relevant industry so as to prepare for morally compromising situations. Job interviews often conclude with the candidate's being asked, "Do you have any questions for me?" A possible response is "What types of ethical dilemmas might be faced in this job?" or "What does this company do to promote ethical business practices?"

Research also shows that elements of a work environment can enhance or diminish self-control, regardless of cultural norms: High uncertainty, excessive cognitive demands, long days and late nights, and consecutive stretch goals all correlate with increased rates of unethical behavior. Such pressures may wax and wane over time in your workplace, but during periods of intensity you should be extra vigilant.

Making Good Decisions

Even if you've planned for an ethical career and established safe-guards, it can be difficult to face moral challenges in the moment. Sometimes people overlook the implications of their decisions—or they find fanciful ways of rationalizing immoral, self-interested behavior. In other instances, they face quandaries in which the right decision isn't obvious—for example, a choice between loyalty to one's coworkers and loyalty to a customer, or a proposed solution that will produce both positive and negative externalities, such as good jobs but also environmental damage. There are several ways to manage moments of truth like these.

First, step back from traditional calculations such as cost-benefit analysis and ROI. Develop a habit of searching for the moral issues and ethical implications at stake in a given decision and analyze them using multiple philosophical perspectives. For instance, from the rule-based perspective of deontology (the study of moral obliga-tion), ask yourself what rules or principles are relevant. Will a certain course of action lead you to violate the principle of being honest or of respecting others? From the consequence-based perspective of utilitarianism, identify potential outcomes for all parties involved or affected either directly or indirectly. What is the greatest good for the greatest number of people? And from the Aristotelian perspec-tive of virtue ethics, ask yourself, Which course of action would best reflect a virtuous person? Each of these philosophies has advantages and disadvantages, but addressing the fundamental decision criteria of all three—rules, consequences, and virtues—will make you less likely to overlook important ethical considerations.

Note, however, that the human mind is skilled at justifying mor-ally questionable behavior when enticed by its benefits. We often tell ourselves things such as "Everyone does this," "I'm just follow-ing my boss's orders," "It's for the greater good," "It's not like I'm robbing a bank," and "It's their own fault—they deserve it." Three tests can help you avoid self-deceptive rationalizations.

1. *The publicity test.* Would you be comfortable having this choice, and your reasoning behind it, published on the front page of the local newspaper?

2. *The generalizability test.* Would you be comfortable having your decision serve as a precedent for all people facing a similar situation?

3. *The mirror test.* Would you like the person you saw in the mirror after making this decision—is that the person you truly want to be?

If the answer to any of these questions is no, think carefully before proceeding.

Studies also show that people are more likely to act unethically if they feel rushed. Very few decisions must be made in the moment. Taking some time for contemplation can help put things in perspective. In a classic social psychology experiment, students at Princeton Theological Seminary were much less likely to stop and help a stranger lying helpless on the ground if they were rushing to get to a lecture they were scheduled to give—on, ironically, the biblical parable of the Good Samaritan, which is about stopping to help a stranger lying helpless on the ground. So be aware of time pressures. Minding the old adage "Sleep on it" can often help you make better moral decisions. And delaying a decision may give you time to consult your ethical mentors. If they are unavailable, practice a variation on the mirror and publicity tests: Imagine explaining your actions to those advisers. If that would make you uncomfortable, be warned.

But taking an ethical stand often requires challenging coworkers or even superiors, which can be excruciatingly difficult. The now infamous Milgram experiments (wherein study participants administered potentially lethal shocks to innocent volunteers when they were instructed to do so by an experimenter) demonstrated how susceptible people can be to pressure from others—especially those in positions of power. How can you avoid succumbing to social pressure? The authors of *The Business Ethics Field Guide* offer a few questions to ask yourself in such situations: Do they have a right to request that I do this? Would others in the organization feel the same way I do about this? What are the requesters trying to accomplish? Could it be accomplished in a different way? Can I refuse to comply in a manner that helps them save face? In general, be wary of doing anything just because "everybody else is doing it" or your boss told you to. Take ownership of your actions.

And don't forget that many ethical challenges people face at work have previously been confronted by others. As a result, companies often develop specific guidelines, protocols, and value statements. If in doubt about a certain situation, try consulting the formal policies of your organization. Does it have an established code of ethics? If not, ask your ethical mentor for guidance. And if you're dealing with something you view as clearly unethical but fear reprisal from a superior, check to see whether your organization has an ombudsman program or a whistle-blowing hotline.

Reflecting After the Fact

Learning from experience is an iterative, lifelong pursuit: A lot of growth happens after decisions are made and actions taken. Ethical people aren't perfect, but when they make mistakes, they review and reflect on them so that they can do better in the future. Indeed, a wide array of research—in fields as diverse as psychology, computer science, nursing, and education—suggests that reflection is a critical first step in learning from past personal experiences. Reflecting on both successes and failures helps people avoid not only repeated transgressions but also "identity segmentation," wherein they compartmentalize their personal and professional lives and perhaps live by a very different moral code in each.

But self-reflection has limitations. Sometimes ethical lapses are obvious; other times the choice is ambiguous. What's more, people can be hemmed in by their own perspectives as well as by their personal histories and biases. That's why we should seek the counsel of people we trust. You can approach this as you would job performance feedback: by asking specific questions, avoiding defensiveness, and expressing gratitude.

Finally, you can engage in what Amy Wrzesniewski of Yale calls *job crafting:* shaping your work experiences by proactively adapting the tasks you undertake, your workplace relationships, and even how you perceive your job, such that work becomes more meaningful and helps you fulfill your potential. You can apply job crafting to your ethical career by making bottom-up changes to your work and the way you approach it that will help you be more virtuous. For example, in some of the earliest studies on job crafting, Wrzesniewski and colleagues found that many hospital housekeepers viewed their work in a way that made them feel like healers, not janitors. They didn't just clean rooms; they helped create a peaceful healing environment. One custodian used her smile and humor to help cancer patients relax and feel more comfortable. She looked for opportunities to interact with them, believing that she could be a momentary bright spot in the darkness of their ongoing chemotherapy. She crafted her job to help her develop and cultivate eulogy virtues such as love, compassion, kindness, and loyalty.

You may feel that it isn't all that difficult to be an ethical professional. As your parents may have told you, just do the right thing. But the evidence suggests that out in the real world it becomes increasingly difficult to remain on the moral high ground. So take control of your ethical career by cultivating moral humility, preparing for challenging situations, maintaining your calm in the moment, and reflecting on how well you've lived up to your values and aspirations.

Originally published in January–February 2020. Reprint R2001L

From Purpose to Impact

Figure out your passion and put it to work.

by Nick Craig and Scott Snook

Over the past five years, there's been an explosion of interest in purpose-driven leadership. Academics argue persuasively that an executive's most important role is to be a steward of the organization's purpose. Business experts make the case that purpose is a key to exceptional performance, while psychologists describe it as the pathway to greater well-being.

Doctors have even found that people with purpose in their lives are less prone to disease. Purpose is increasingly being touted as the key to navigating the complex, volatile, ambiguous world we face today, where strategy is ever changing and few decisions are obviously right or wrong.

Despite this growing understanding, however, a big challenge remains. In our work training thousands of managers at organizations from GE to the Girl Scouts, and teaching an equal number of executives and students at Harvard Business School, we've found that fewer than 20% of leaders have a strong sense of their own individual purpose. Even fewer can distill their purpose into a concrete statement. They may be able to clearly articulate their organization's mission: Think of Google's "To organize the world's information and make it universally accessible and useful," or Charles Schwab's "A relentless ally for the individual investor." But when asked to describe their own purpose, they typically fall back on something generic and nebulous: "Help others excel." "Ensure success." "Empower my people." Just as problematic, hardly any of them have a clear plan for translating purpose into action. As a result, they limit their aspirations and often fail to achieve their most ambitious professional and personal goals.

Our purpose is to change that—to help executives find and define their leadership purpose and put it to use. Building on the seminal work of our colleague Bill George, our programs initially covered a wide range of topics related to authentic leadership, but in recent years purpose has emerged as the cornerstone of our teaching and coaching. Executives tell us it is the key to accelerating their growth and deepening their impact, in both their professional and personal lives. Indeed, we believe that the process of articulating your purpose and finding the courage to live it—what we call *purpose to impact*—is the single most important developmental task you can undertake as a leader.

Consider Dolf van den Brink, the president and CEO of Heineken USA. Working with us, he identified a decidedly unique purpose statement—"To be the wuxia master who saves the kingdom"—which reflects his love of Chinese kung fu movies, the inspiration he takes from the wise, skillful warriors in them, and the realization that he, too, revels in high-risk situations that compel him to take action. With that impetus, he was able to create a plan for reviving a challenged legacy business during extremely difficult economic conditions. We've also watched a retail operations chief call on his newly clarified purpose—"Compelled to make things better, whomever, wherever, however"—to make the "hard, cage-rattling changes" needed to beat back a global competitor. And we've seen a factory director in Egypt use his purpose—"Create families that excel"—to persuade employees that they should honor the 2012 protest movement not by joining the marches but by maintaining their loyalties to one another and keeping their shared operation running.

We've seen similar results outside the corporate world. Kathi Snook (Scott's wife) is a retired army colonel who'd been struggling to reengage in work after several years as a stay-at-home mom. But after nailing her purpose statement—"To be the gentle, behind-the-scenes,

Idea in Brief

The Problem

Purpose is increasingly seen as the key to navigating the complex world we face today, where strategy is ever changing and few decisions are obviously right or wrong. At the same time, few leaders have a strong sense of their own leadership purpose or a clear plan for translating it into action. As a result, they often fail to achieve their most ambitious professional and personal goals.

The Solution

The first step toward uncovering your leadership purpose is to mine your life story for major themes that reveal your lifelong passions and values. Next, craft a concise purpose statement that leaves you emboldened and energized. Finally, develop a *purpose-to-impact plan*. Effective plans:

- Use language that is uniquely meaningful to you

- Focus on big-picture aspirations and then set shorter-term goals, working backward with increasing specificity

- Emphasize the strengths you bring to the table

- Take a holistic view of work and family

kick-in-the-ass reason for success," something she'd done throughout her military career and with her kids—she decided to run for a hotly contested school committee seat, and won.

And we've implemented this thinking across organizations. Unilever is a company that is committed to purpose-driven leadership, and Jonathan Donner, the head of global learning there, has been a key partner in refining our approach. Working with his company and several other organizations, we've helped more than 1,000 leaders through the purpose-to-impact process and have begun to track and review their progress over the past two to three years. Many have seen dramatic results, ranging from two-step promotions to sustained improvement in business results. Most important, the vast majority tell us they've developed a new ability to thrive in even the most challenging times.

In this article, we share our step-by-step framework to start you down the same path. We'll explain how to identify your purpose and then develop an impact plan to achieve concrete results.

What Is Purpose?

Your leadership purpose is who you are and what makes you distinctive. Whether you're an entrepreneur at a start-up or the CEO of a *Fortune* 500 company, a call center rep or a software developer, your purpose is your brand, what you're driven to achieve, the magic that makes you tick. It's not *what* you do, it's *how* you do your job and *why*—the strengths and passions you bring to the table no matter where you're seated. Although you may express your purpose in different ways in different contexts, it's what everyone close to you recognizes as uniquely you and would miss most if you were gone.

When Kathi shared her purpose statement with her family and friends, the response was instantaneous and overwhelming: "Yes! That's you—all business, all the time!" In every role and every context—as captain of the army gymnastics team, as a math teacher at West Point, informally with her family and friends—she had always led from behind, a gentle but forceful catalyst for others' success. Through this new lens, she was able to see herself—and her future—more clearly. When Dolf van den Brink revealed his newly articulated purpose to his wife, she easily recognized the "wuxia master" who had led his employees through the turmoil of serious fighting and unrest in the Congo and was now ready to attack the challenges at Heineken USA head-on.

At its core, your leadership purpose springs from your identity, the essence of who you are. Purpose is not a list of the education, experience, and skills you've gathered in your life. We'll use ourselves as examples: The fact that Scott is a retired army colonel with an MBA and a PhD is not his purpose. His purpose is "to help others live more 'meaning-full' lives." Purpose is also not a professional title, limited to your current job or organization. Nick's purpose is not "To lead the Authentic Leadership Institute." That's his job. His purpose is "To wake you up and have you find that you are home." He has been doing just that since he was a teenager, and if you sit next to him on the shuttle from Boston to New York, he'll wake you up (figuratively), too. He simply can't help himself.

Purpose is definitely not some jargon-filled catch-all ("Empower my team to achieve exceptional business results while delighting our customers"). It should be specific and personal, resonating with you and you alone. It doesn't have to be aspirational or cause-based ("Save the whales" or "Feed the hungry"). And it's not what you think it should be. It's who you can't help being. In fact, it might not necessarily be all that flattering ("Be the thorn in people's side that keeps them moving!").

How Do You Find It?

Finding your leadership purpose is not easy. If it were, we'd all know exactly why we're here and be living that purpose every minute of every day. We are constantly bombarded by powerful messages (from parents, bosses, management gurus, advertisers, celebrities) about what we should be (smarter, stronger, richer) and about how to lead (empower others, lead from behind, be authentic, distribute power). To figure out who you are in such a world, let alone "be nobody but yourself," is indeed hard work. However, our experience shows that when you have a clear sense of who you are, everything else follows naturally.

Some people will come to the purpose-to-impact journey with a natural bent toward introspection and reflection. Others will find the experience uncomfortable and anxiety-provoking. A few will just roll their eyes. We've worked with leaders of all stripes and can attest that even the most skeptical discover personal and professional value in the experience. At one multinational corporation, we worked with a senior lawyer who characterized himself as "the least likely person to ever find this stuff useful." Yet he became such a supporter that he required all his people to do the program. "I have never read a self-help book, and I don't plan to," he told his staff. "But if you want to become an exceptional leader, you have to know your leadership purpose." The key to engaging both the dreamers and the skeptics is to build a process that has room to express individuality but also offers step-by-step practical guidance.

The first task is to mine your life story for common threads and major themes. The point is to identify your core, lifelong strengths, values, and passions—those pursuits that energize you and bring you joy. We use a variety of prompts but have found three to be most effective:

- What did you especially love doing when you were a child, before the world told you what you should or shouldn't like or do? Describe a moment and how it made you feel.

- Tell us about two of your most challenging life experiences. How have they shaped you?

- What do you enjoy doing in your life now that helps you sing your song?

We strongly recommend grappling with these questions in a small group of a few peers, because we've found that it's almost impossible for people to identify their leadership purpose by themselves. You can't get a clear picture of yourself without trusted colleagues or friends to act as mirrors.

After this reflective work, take a shot at crafting a clear, concise, and declarative statement of purpose: "My leadership purpose is _____." The words in your purpose statement must be yours. They must capture your essence. And they must call you to action.

To give you an idea of how the process works, consider the experiences of a few executives. When we asked one manager about her childhood passions, she told us about growing up in rural Scotland and delighting in "discovery" missions. One day, she and a friend set out determined to find frogs and spent the whole day going from pond to pond, turning over every stone. Just before dark, she discovered a single frog and was triumphant. The purpose statement she later crafted—"Always find the frogs!"—is perfect for her current role as the senior VP of R&D for her company.

Another executive used two "crucible" life experiences to craft her purpose. The first was personal: Years before, as a divorced young mother of two, she found herself homeless and begging on the street, but she used her wits to get back on her feet. The second was professional: During the economic crisis of 2008, she had to oversee her company's retrenchment from Asia and was tasked with closing the flagship operation in the region. Despite the near hopeless job environment, she was able to help every one of her employees find another job before letting them go. After discussing these stories with her group, she shifted her purpose statement from "Continually and consistently develop and facilitate the growth and development of myself and others leading to great performance" to "With tenacity, create brilliance."

Dolf came to his "wuxia master" statement after exploring not only his film preferences but also his extraordinary crucible experience in the Congo, when militants were threatening the brewery he managed and he had to order it barricaded to protect his employees and prevent looting. The Egyptian factory director focused on family as his purpose because his stories revealed that familial love and support had been the key to facing every challenge in his life, while the retail operations chief used "Compelled to improve" after realizing that his greatest achievements had always come when he pushed himself and others out of their comfort zones.

As you review your stories, you will see a unifying thread, just as these executives did. Pull it, and you'll uncover your purpose. (The exhibit "Purpose Statements: From Bad to Good" offers sampling of purpose statements.)

How Do You Put Your Purpose into Action?

Clarifying your purpose as a leader is critical, but writing the statement is not enough. You must also envision the impact you'll have on your world as a result of living your purpose. Your actions—not your words—are what really matter. Of course, it's virtually impossible for any of us to fully live into our purpose 100% of the time. But with work and careful planning, we can do it more often, more consciously, wholeheartedly, and effectively.

Purpose-to-impact plans differ from traditional development plans in several important ways: They start with a statement of leadership purpose rather than of a business or career goal. They take a

Purpose statements

From bad . . .	To good	Purpose-to-impact planning	Traditional development planning
Lead new markets department to achieve exceptional business results	Eliminate "chaos"	Uses meaningful, purpose-infused language	Uses standard business language
Be a driver in the infrastructure business that allows each person to achieve their needed outcomes while also mastering the new drivers of our business as I balance my family and work demands	Bring water and power to the 2 billion people who do not have it	Is focused on strengths to realize career aspirations	Is focused on weaknesses to address performance
Continually and consistently develop and facilitate the growth and development of myself and others leading to great performance	With tenacity, create brilliance	Elicits a statement of leadership purpose that explains how you will lead	States a business- or career-driven goal
		Sets incremental goals related to living your leadership purpose	Measures success using metrics tied to the firm's mission and goals
		Focuses on the future, working backward	Focuses on the present, working forward
		Is unique to you; addresses who you are as a leader	Is generic; addresses the job or role
		Takes a holistic view of work and family	Ignores goals and responsibilities outside the office

holistic view of professional and personal life rather than ignore the fact that you have a family or outside interests and commitments. They incorporate meaningful, purpose-infused language to create a document that speaks to you, not just to any person in your job or role. They force you to envision long-term opportunities for living your purpose (three to five years out) and then help you to work backward from there (two years out, one year, six months, three months, 30 days) to set specific goals for achieving them.

When executives approach development in this purpose-driven way, their aspirations—for instance, Kathi's decision to get involved in the school board, or the Egyptian factory director's ambition to run manufacturing and logistics across the Middle East—are stoked. Leaders also become more energized in their current roles. Dolf's impact plan inspired him to tackle his role at Heineken USA with four mottos for his team: "Be brave," "Decide and do," "Hunt as a pack," and "Take it personally." When Unilever executive Jostein Solheim created a development plan around his purpose—"To be part of a global movement that makes changing the world seem fun and achievable"—he realized he wanted to stay on as CEO of the Ben & Jerry's business rather than moving up the corporate ladder.

Let's now look at a hypothetical purpose-to-impact plan (representing a composite of several people with whom we've worked) for an in-depth view of the process. "Richard" arrived at his purpose only after being prodded into talking about his lifelong passion for sailing; suddenly, he'd found a set of experiences and language that could redefine how he saw his job in procurement.

Richard's development plan leads with the **PURPOSE STATEMENT** he crafted: "To harness all the elements to win the race." This is followed by **AN EXPLANATION** of why that's his purpose: Research shows that understanding what motivates us dramatically increases our ability to achieve big goals.

Next, Richard addresses his **THREE- TO FIVE-YEAR GOALS** using the language of his purpose statement. We find that this is a good time frame to target first; several years is long enough that even the

A Purpose-to-Impact Plan

THIS SAMPLE PLAN SHOWS HOW "Richard" uses his unique leadership purpose to envision big-picture aspirations and then work backward to set more-specific goals.

1. Create Purpose Statement

To harness all the elements to win the race

2. Write Explanation

I love to sail. In my teens and 20s, I raced high-performance three-man skiffs and almost made it to the Olympics. Now sailing is my hobby and passion— a challenge that requires discipline, balance, and coordination. You never know what the wind will do next, and in the end, you win the race only by relying on your team's combined capabilities, intuition, and flow. It's all about how you read the elements.

3. Set Three- to Five-Year Goals

Be known for training the best crews and winning the big races: Take on a global procurement role and use the opportunity to push my organization ahead of competitors

How Will I Do It?

- Make everyone feel they're part of the same team
- Navigate unpredictable conditions by seeing wind shears before everyone else
- Keep calm when we lose individual races; learn and prepare for the next ones

Celebrate my shore team: Make sure the family has one thing we do that binds us

4. Set Two-Year Goals

Win the gold: Implement a new procurement model, redefining our relationship with suppliers and generating 10% cost savings for the company

Tackle next-level racing challenge: Move into a European role with broader responsibilities

How Will I Do It?

- Anticipate and then face the tough challenges
- Insist on innovative yet rigorous and pragmatic solutions
- Assemble and train the winning crew

Develop my shore team: Teach the boys to sail

5. Set One-Year Goals

Target the gold: Begin to develop new procurement process

Win the short race: Deliver Sympix project ahead of expectations

Build a seaworthy boat: Keep TFLS process within cost and cash forecast

How Will I Do It?
- Accelerate team reconfiguration
- Get buy-in from management for new procurement approach

Invest in my shore team: Take a two-week vacation, no email

6. Map Out Critical Next Steps

Assemble the crew: Finalize key hires

Chart the course: Lay the groundwork for Sympix and TFLS projects

How Will I Do It?
Six Months:
- Finalize succession plans
- Set out Sympix timeline

Three Months:
- Land a world-class replacement for Jim
- Schedule "action windows" to focus with no email

30 Days:
- Bring Alex in Shanghai on board
- Agree on TFLS metrics
- Conduct one-day Sympix offsite

Reconnect with my shore team: Be more present with Jill and the boys

7. Examine Key Relationships

Sarah, HR manager

Jill, manager of my "shore team"

most disillusioned managers could imagine they'd actually be living into their purpose by then. But it's not so distant that it creates complacency. A goal might be to land a top job—in Richard's case, a global procurement role—but the focus should be on how you will do it, what kind of leader you'll be.

Then he considers TWO-YEAR GOALS. This is a time frame in which the grand future and current reality begin to merge. What new responsibilities will you take on? What do you have to do to set yourself up for the longer term? Remember to address your personal life, too, because you should be more fully living into your purpose everywhere. Richard's goals explicitly reference his family, or "shore team."

The fifth step—setting ONE-YEAR GOALS—is often the most challenging. Many people ask, "What if most of what I am doing today isn't aligned in any way with my leadership purpose? How do I get from here to there?" We've found two ways to address this problem. First, think about whether you can rewrite the narrative on parts of your work, or change the way you do some tasks, so that they become an expression of your purpose. For example, the phrase "seaworthy boat" helps Richard see the meaning in managing a basic procurement process. Second, consider whether you can add an activity that is 100% aligned with your purpose. We've found that most people can manage to devote 5% to 10% of their time to something that energizes them and helps others see their strengths. Take Richard's decision to contribute to the global strategic procurement effort: It's not part of his "day job," but it gets him involved in a more purpose-driven project.

Now we get to the nitty-gritty. What are the CRITICAL NEXT STEPS that you must take in the coming six months, three months, and 30 days to accomplish the one-year goals you've set out? The importance of small wins is well documented in almost every management discipline from change initiatives to innovation. In detailing your next steps, don't write down all the requirements of your job. List the activities or results that are most critical given your newly clarified leadership purpose and ambitions. You'll probably notice that a number of your tasks seem much less urgent than they did before, while others you had pushed to the side take priority.

Finally, we look at the **KEY RELATIONSHIPS** needed to turn your plan into reality. Identify two or three people who can help you live more fully into your leadership purpose. For Richard, it is Sarah, the HR manager who will help him assemble his crew, and his wife, Jill, the manager of his "shore team."

Executives tell us that their individual purpose-to-impact plans help them stay true to their short-and long-term goals, inspiring courage, commitment, and focus. When they're frustrated or flagging, they pull out the plans to remind themselves what they want to accomplish and how they'll succeed. After creating his plan, the retail operations chief facing global competition said he's no longer "shying away from things that are too hard." Dolf van den Brink said: "I'm much clearer on where I really can contribute and where not. I have full clarity on the kind of roles I aspire to and can make explicit choices along the way."

What creates the greatest leaders and companies? Each of them operates from a slightly different set of assumptions about the world, their industry, what can or can't be done. That individual perspective allows them to create great value and have significant impact. They all operate with a unique leadership purpose. To be a truly effective leader, you must do the same. Clarify your purpose, and put it to work.

Originally published in May 2014. Reprint R1405H

About the Contributors

MORRA AARONS-MELE is the author of *The Anxious Achiever* (Harvard Business Review Press, 2023). She has written for the *New York Times*, the *Wall Street Journal, O the Oprah Magazine,* and other publications, and is the host of the *Anxious Achiever* podcast from LinkedIn Presents. Follow her on Twitter @morraam.

ROBIN ABRAHAMS is a research associate at Harvard Business School.

CHRIS ANDERSON is the curator of TED.

BILL BIRCHARD is a business writer and writing coach. His newest book is *Writing for Impact*. His previous books include *Merchants of Virtue, Stairway to Earth, Nature's Keepers,* and *Counting What Counts*. Learn more about the craft of writing at billbirchard.com.

MARCUS BUCKINGHAM is the head of people and performance research at the ADP Research Institute and a coauthor of *Nine Lies About Work* (Harvard Business Review Press, 2019). His most recent book is *Love + Work* (Harvard Business Review Press, 2022).

BRIANNA BARKER CAZA is a PhD candidate in organizational psychology at the University of Michigan.

ROBERT B. CIALDINI is the Regents' Professor of Psychology at Arizona State University and the author of *Influence*, now in its fourth edition. Further regularly updated information about the influence process can be found at www.influenceatwork.com.

NICK CRAIG is the president of the Authentic Leadership Institute.

KEITH D. DORSEY is a managing partner and the U.S. practice leader of CEO and board services at Boyden, a global executive search firm with 75 offices in 45 countries. He is a researcher, author, advisor, and active board member at Vimly Benefit Solutions, Pepperdine

University's Graziadio Business School, and the City of La Quinta's Financial Advisory Commission.

NANCY DUARTE is a bestselling author with thirty years of CEO-ing under her belt. She's driven her firm, Duarte, Inc., to be the global leader behind some of the most influential messages and visuals in business and culture. Duarte, Inc., is the largest design firm in Silicon Valley, as well as one of the top woman-owned businesses in the area. Nancy has written six bestselling books; four have won awards. Her most recent book is *DataStory*. Follow her on Twitter @nancyduarte.

JANE DUTTON is the Robert L. Kahn Distinguished University Professor of Business Administration and Psychology at the University of Michigan's Ross School of Business. She is cofounder of the Center for Positive Organizations at Ross.

JOSEPH FULLER is a professor of management practice and a faculty cochair of the Project on Managing the Future of Work at Harvard Business School. He also cochairs Harvard's Project on Workforce, a collaboration among members of the faculty at the university's schools of business, education, and government.

ASHLEY GOODALL is the senior vice president of leadership and team intelligence at Cisco Systems. He is coauthor of *Nine Lies About Work* (Harvard Business Review Press, 2019).

BORIS GROYSBERG is a professor of business administration in the Organizational Behavior unit at Harvard Business School and a faculty affiliate at the school's Race, Gender & Equity Initiative. He is the coauthor, with Colleen Ammerman, of *Glass Half-Broken: Shattering the Barriers That Still Hold Women Back at Work* (Harvard Business Review Press, 2021). Follow him on Twitter @bgroysberg.

STEPHEN HANSEN is an associate professor of economics at Imperial College Business School.

EMILY HEAPHY is an assistant professor of management at the Isenberg School of Management at the University of Massachusetts Amherst.

HERMINIA IBARRA is the Charles Handy Professor of Organizational Behavior at London Business School and the author of *Act Like a Leader, Think Like a Leader, Updated Edition of the Global Bestseller* (Harvard Business Review Press, 2023) and *Working Identity, Updated Edition* (Harvard Business Review Press, 2023). Follow her on Twitter @HerminiaIbarra.

MARYAM KOUCHAKI is a professor of management and organizations at the Kellogg School of Management.

PJ NEAL is the global head of knowledge and operations for the Board & CEO Advisory Group at Russell Reynolds Associates.

ROBERT QUINN is a professor emeritus at the University of Michigan's Ross School of Business and a cofounder of the school's Center for Positive Organizations.

LAURA MORGAN ROBERTS is an organizational psychologist, the Frank M. Sands Sr. Associate Professor of Business Administration at the University of Virginia's Darden School of Business, and the coeditor of *Race, Work, and Leadership: New Perspectives on the Black Experience* (Harvard Business Review Press, 2019).

RAFFAELLA SADUN is the Charles E. Wilson professor of business administration at Harvard Business School.

ISAAC H. SMITH is an assistant professor of organizational behavior and human resources at BYU Marriott School of Business. His research explores the morality and ethics of organizations and the people in them.

SCOTT SNOOK is an associate professor of organizational behavior at Harvard Business School. He served in the U.S. Army Corps of Engineers for over 22 years.

GRETCHEN SPREITZER is the Keith E. and Valerie J. Alessi Professor of Business Administration at the University of Michigan's Ross School of Business, where she is a core faculty member in the Center for Positive Organizations. Her most recent work looks at positive deviance and how organizations enable employees to thrive.

Index

job, redesigning, 80–81
patterns, recognizing, 76–78
self-portrait, 78–80
reciprocity, persuasion and, 20, 22–24
relocation, work/life balance and, 9–10
research, work/life balance, 12
résumé virtues, 136
Roberts, Laura Morgan, 71–82
ruminating, anxiety and, 66
Russell Reynolds studies, 122, 124

Sadun, Raffaella, 121–133
scarcity, persuasion and, 21, 31–32
self-centeredness, feedback theories and, 93
self-deceptive rationalizations, 140
generalizability test, 141
mirror test, 141
publicity test, 141
self-reflection, ethics and, 142–143
sense of self, authenticity and, 109
should statements, anxiety and, 64–65
similarities, persuasion and, 18–20
Smith, Isaac H., 135–143
Snook, Kathi, 146, 148
Snook, Scott, 145–157
Snyder, Mark, 110
social comparison, anxiety and, 65
social content, writing skills, 55–56
social influence, ethics and, 33
social proof, persuasion and, 20
social skills, C-suite, 123–125
access, 130–131
collective, 132
complexity and, 126
diversity and inclusion, 128
executive development programs, 120–121
firm size, 126

information-processing technologies, 126–127
networking and, 127–128
social media and, 127–128
source of truth, 92
abstract qualities and, 94
idiosyncratic rater effect, 94
random error and, 94
systematic error and, 94
Spreitzer, Gretchen, 71–82
strengths, playing to, 71–72
POS (positive organizational scholarship), 72
RBS (Reflected Best Self), 72–74
success, defining for oneself, 2–6
support networks, work/life balance and, 8–9
systematic error, feedback and, 94

technology, work/life balance and, 5–8
TED Talks
teleprompters, 40–41
Turere, Richard, 35–36
text messages, work/life balance, 5–8
Thatcher, Margaret, 114
theory of mind, 123
thinking errors, 60
thought traps, 60
anxiety
all-or-nothing thinking, 60–61
blaming, 65–66
catastrophizing, 63
discounting positive aspects, 64
emotional reasoning, 66–67
filtering, 63–64
jumping to conclusions, 62–63
labeling, 61–62
personalization, 65–66
ruminating, 66